101 Ways to Save America (Before It's Too Late)

101 Ways to Save America (Before It's Too Late)

❖   ❖   ❖

Timothy M. Rosen

ISBN: 0692706860
ISBN 13: 9780692706862
Library of Congress Control Number: 2016908142
Patriot's Press, New York, NY

For My Grandmother
She loved people, she loved freedom, and boy did she love America!

INTRODUCTION

Do you love America? Do you believe that the values of America are the best hope for the human race? This book is being written because America has lost her way. We are not what we used to be. The great patriots of times past bequeathed to us an inheritance that is now being stolen. For the sake of those patriots who came before us, for the sake of our posterity, and for our own sake, we must act now to save America. In short, America as we know it is being destroyed. Our liberty is being destroyed. Our traditional values are being destroyed. Our borders, language, and schools are all being destroyed. Our Constitution is being destroyed. The list is endless. America is still a great nation but she has gone off course and if we are to save America we must start putting her back on the right course—and *fast*. There really is no time to lose! If we don't act decisively and act fast it will soon be too late to act at all. The damage will become irreversible.

America as we know it will soon cease to exist. Yes, the country will still be here, but America will be virtually un-recognizable—a pathetic shadow of her former glory.

If you love America and believe America is worth saving then this book is for you. This book is written for the patriot who still loves America and knows that she is well worth saving. What must we save? We must save our liberty, our language, our borders, our courts, our schools, our traditional values, our economy, our middle-class, and our Constitution. In short, we must save America! I hope that this book will, in some small way, inspire others to save America. I'm certainly no great writer or great speaker and I'm not a great genius either. I'm just a regular American who loves his country and still believes it can be and should be that "shining city upon a hill." This book, for whatever it's worth, is being written because it pains me to see my country go down the drain and I want to do something about it—before it's too late!

Will you agree with all the 101 ideas in this book? No, probably not. If you're an intelligent person who thinks for yourself you may agree with some of the ideas contained herein and you may disagree with others. We're Americans. We think for ourselves. We're not robots. Washington, Adams, and Jefferson didn't always see eye to eye. Reasonable people can disagree about all sorts of things but the main thing is love of country. If you love America and want to save America then this book is meant for you. Take from it what you will. Pick and choose what makes sense to you and what doesn't. If you happen to be a liberal, many of the ideas in this book will probably make you sick to your stomach. That's fine. Pick and choose and perhaps find some ideas that make more sense to you. On the other hand, not all of these ideas will go over well with ardent conservatives or libertarians either.

It should also be noted that my ideas, thoughts, and beliefs are still evolving and subject to revision. It would be arrogant of anyone to think that they alone have all the answers and know what is best for a nation. These ideas are simply my best efforts based on what I know right now. Some of these suggestions may prove to be unwise but they represent this writer's best efforts and above all, they are from the heart. In the end, this book is about love—love of God, love of people, love of freedom (which is a gift from God), and of course, love of country. I love the United States of America. I'm not ashamed of that—I'm proud of it. We must save this country because America is the "land of the free" and it is the "last best hope" for all of God's children. It is my fervent hope and prayer that this book might serve as a modest contribution to inspire others to make America a better country, to restore America's values, traditions, and culture, and to try to save America as we know it, for both ourselves and our posterity. America is worth saving. Now let's get to work!

1

SECURE THE BORDER

A nation that can't control its own borders is not fit to be called a nation. For decades now, America's southern border has been overrun by millions of illegal immigrants. We now have over 11-12 million illegal immigrants living in the United States. To be sure, many of these people are simply coming here out of desperation, trying to escape extreme poverty and make a better life. We ought to have compassion for them and for their plight. In fact, if any of us were born into poverty in Mexico, we would most likely try to jump the border ourselves! We shouldn't look down upon these people or denigrate them for no matter what nation we're born in, we're all God's children. Yes, we ought to have compassion for them but we can't allow our sense of compassion to lead to the downfall of our country. There are billions of poor people all over the world who wish they could get into the United States. Who can blame them? But our nation simply cannot absorb even a fraction of all the people that want to come here. We have no choice. We must put the American people first. We *must* secure the border! We must not only secure it but seal it off completely, once and for all.

Yes, on this one issue Donald Trump is right. We need to build a wall. In 2006, Congress passed the Secure Fence Act which called for building a secure, double-layered fence along 700 miles of America's southern border. First of all, the 700 miles of double-layered fencing that the law called for has not even been fully completed. It needs to be fully completed but even that is not enough. 700 miles of fencing is a good start but it's not good enough. The U.S. border with Mexico stretches 2,000 miles from California to Texas. We need a secure fence that runs the entire length of that border. It should be as high and as thick as necessary. It should be double-layered with razor and barbed wire—whatever it takes to put a *complete* stop to all illegal crossings. We should also double or even triple the size of the border patrol and use the military if necessary—whatever it takes! We must secure the border at all costs. Any nation that can't or won't control its own borders will eventually be overrun and cease to exist as a sovereign country. There are already 11 to 12 million illegal aliens here. What if we do nothing? What if we just allow the southern border to remain wide open? Eventually instead of 11-12 million illegal aliens there will be 22-24 million. When would it stop? When America as we know it ceases to exist? When the entire southwestern portion of the United States secedes from the Union and reverts back to Mexico? Think it can't happen?

The government of Mexico has been aiding and abetting illegal immigrants for many years. They actively encourage their citizens to violate American sovereignty and even give them tips on how to cross the border and evade capture. The Mexican government does not respect American sovereignty in the least and that's not an exaggeration. Former Mexican President Felipe Calderon was quite clear about it when he said the following: "I have said that Mexico does not stop at its border, that wherever there is a Mexican there is Mexico." Another former Mexican president, Vincente Fox, had the audacity to call our efforts to build a fence on our own border, "shameful." It's worth noting that in recent years almost 70% of illegal immigrants have been from Mexico or countries in Central America. It is also worth noting that under Mexican law it is a felony to enter illegally into Mexico and those who do so are swiftly deported or thrown in jail.

It's high time that we stand up to Mexico and to the lunatic liberals on the Left as well as the corporate interests on the Right, all of whom want open borders. We must fully secure our borders—no more half-hearted measures. We must spend whatever amount of money is necessary and just get the job done once and for all. Just do it! No more excuses. Without a border we are not fit to be called sovereign country. If our borders continue to remain porous, eventually America as we know it will disintegrate. We can't allow that to happen. Build that fence and secure the border *now!*

2

MAKE IT A FELONY TO HIRE
ILLEGAL IMMIGRANTS

Most illegal immigrants come here for work. It's quite simple really. There is a demand for their labor and so they come here to supply that demand. If you cut off the demand they will no longer come. The easiest and simplest way to cut off the demand for illegal immigrant labor is to swiftly and severely punish the employers who hire them. It is the employers that create the demand. Cut off the demand and the illegal immigrants stop coming, it's just that simple. In addition to that, many of the ones already here will return home of their own accord. If employers know that there is a very good chance they'll end up in prison for hiring illegal immigrants they will no longer do so. For too long we have focused on the illegal immigrants—who are just looking for work—rather than on the employers who hire them. It's time for that to change. A law should be passed that makes it a federal criminal offense to knowingly hire an illegal immigrant. Anyone caught doing so will be guilty of a felony punishable by not less than one year in jail. In addition, anyone who doesn't diligently verify the legal status of their employees, and thus negligently hires an illegal immigrant, will be guilty of a misdemeanor punishable by not less than six months in jail.

3

FULLY INSTITUTE THE "E-VERIFY" SYSTEM AND MAKE IT MANDATORY

E-Verify is a system that allows employers to quickly and easily check on the legal status of employees. They can usually check on a person's status within a matter of seconds. It's a terrific system that can really help put a stop to illegal immigration. The only problem with E-Verify is that not enough people are using it. Only a small percentage of employers are legally required to use it and for the rest it's voluntary. That needs to change. We need to pass a federal law that requires *all* employers to check the immigration status of their employees by using the E-Verify system. If an employer willfully refuses to use the E-Verify system and subsequently is caught employing illegal immigrants, that employer should be prosecuted and thrown in jail.

4

FINGERPRINT AND PHOTOGRAPH EVERY SINGLE PERSON COMING INTO OUR COUNTRY

America is a gigantic country of over 320 million people and we need to do a much better job of keeping track of who is coming and who is going. A substantial number of illegal immigrants do not come here by simply jumping the fence at our southern border. About 40% of them come here legally and then just overstay their visas. We need to do everything possible to keep close tabs on those who come here. We ought to fingerprint and photograph every single visitor coming into the country and then create a biometric database. This will make it easier to track down people who overstay their visas. It will also help keep track of potential terrorists! People forget that at least two of the 9/11 terrorists were here in violation of our immigration laws.

5

TRACK DOWN AND DEPORT ANYONE WHO OVERSTAYS THEIR VISA

As previously stated, many people come here legally at first and then just overstay their visas. Once we have created a biometric database of all visitors, we need to do a much better job of finding and deporting people who illegally remain here long after their visas have expired. The Department of Homeland Security should be provided with all the resources necessary to find and deport all such people and this type of enforcement must be given a high priority. In addition, we need to be much more careful about who we issue visas to in the first place. One of the Jihadist maniacs who slaughtered innocent people in San Bernardino was here on a visa. The Department of State should not just issue a visa to anyone. They should first have to undergo a rigorous background check and provide references.

They should also have to demonstrate that they have no intention of overstaying their visa and if they do they must be tracked down and swiftly deported.

6

ENCOURAGE LOCAL LAW ENFORCEMENT TO HELP TRACK DOWN ILLEGAL IMMIGRANTS

When the people of Arizona tried to help enforce federal immigration laws President Obama sued them. Instead of suing them Obama should have thanked them! Instead of trying to handicap state and local law enforcement, the federal government should actively seek out their help. The federal government can't do everything thing on its own. We have a myriad of state, county, and local law enforcement agencies that can and should assist the federal government in the enforcement of our immigration laws.

7

CUT OFF ALL FUNDING TO SANCTUARY CITIES

Any city, county, or state that willfully ignores or seeks to subvert federal immigration laws should have *all* federal funds cut off. These "sanctuary cities" that refuse to cooperate with federal enforcement efforts should not get one dime in federal funds—not one dime! In major cities all over the country lunatic liberals have passed laws and signed executive orders that prevent law enforcement from inquiring as to the immigration status of criminal suspects. A law was passed in New York City that now orders the New York Police Department and the New York Department of Correction to refuse to cooperate with federal immigration authorities. Most criminal aliens who would otherwise be transferred to federal authorities for deportation are now simply released back onto the streets of New York City and similar cities all across America.

This insanity has had tragic consequences. A young woman, Kathryn Steinle, was gunned down on the streets of San Francisco by an illegal immigrant from Mexico. Juan Francisco Lopez-Sanchez had a record of seven felony convictions and had been previously deported not once, not twice, but five times. In spite of this, the utterly insane liberals in San Francisco decided to adhere to their "sanctuary city" policy and released him back onto the streets where he murdered this innocent young woman. These lunatic liberals have Kate Steinle's blood on their hands but they don't care. They have their insane ideology and they will stick with it no matter how many innocent people are killed or maimed.

Some states are now even giving driver's licenses to illegal immigrants. The Supreme Court of California even declared that illegal immigrants must be allowed to become attorneys and practice law! Can you believe that? All of this is madness, pure madness. These cities and states should be punished for their deliberate subversion of our immigration laws. Not only should federal funds be cut off but these cities and states should also be sued in federal court. Obama sued Arizona for trying to *help* the federal government enforce the law. But has he or any of his liberal cohorts sued these sanctuary cities and states that are willfully and deliberately undermining federal immigration law? It's time to end this madness.

8

PASS THE DREAM ACT

Children should not be held accountable for the actions of their parents. To do so is unjust and unfair. Some will object and call this amnesty, and they're right, it *is* amnesty. But it's not amnesty for all illegal immigrants, just for those who came here when they were children. The so-called "Dream Act" would grant citizenship to young people who came here as children and have stayed out of trouble. Do we really want to deport an 18 year old kid who was brought here when he was a baby, has never committed a crime, speaks English fluently, and loves baseball and apple pie? To do such a thing would be downright un-American! We must pass the Dream Act and not punish children for the actions of their parents. These kids are Americans in spirit, if not in law, and we should grant them full citizenship. It's just the right thing to do. However, one caveat: We also need to get rid of chain-migration. Just because these kids get citizenship should not mean they get to bring over their whole extended families.

While discussing the Dream Act it should also be noted that President Obama's executive order known as Deferred Action for Childhood Arrivals—DACA—was a totally unconstitutional abuse of power. Yes, we ought to grant these kids the right to remain here but it must be done the proper way—the constitutional way. A president does not have the legal authority to just rewrite federal immigration laws with the stroke of his pen. He is a president, not a dictator! If the Dream Act is to be passed— and let's hope it is—it must be passed by the Congress.

9

ALLOW SOME ILLEGAL IMMIGRANTS TO STAY BUT NO CITIZENSHIP

First and foremost, we must *totally* secure our borders. Until our borders are totally 100% secured we should not even consider what to do about the illegal aliens that are here. But when and if our borders are finally secured, what should we do with the 11-12 million illegal aliens that are already here? Should we round them all up and deport them or should we grant them all full citizenship? Perhaps the answer is somewhere in the middle. Many of us take pride in the Judeo-Christian tradition that is so inextricably intertwined with the history of our country. A cornerstone of that tradition is the paramount importance of compassion, love, and mercy for all of God's children. Yes, the 11-12 million illegal aliens who have come here are guilty of breaking our laws but we still ought to have compassion upon them. Perhaps some of them were just trying to make a better life for themselves and who can blame them for that? If you or I were born into poverty in some corrupt backwater Mexican town, we might very well be illegal immigrants ourselves! So no, we should not attempt to deport all of these illegal immigrants; however, neither should we reward them with citizenship. Other than those who were brought here as children, no illegal immigrant should be granted citizenship. Perhaps some should eventually be granted some kind of legal status but why reward them with the privilege of citizenship when they have cut the line in front of all the immigrants who came here lawfully?

So what should we do? It's pretty simple. We should deport some of them and leave some of them alone. First of all, any illegal immigrant that has been convicted of a crime should be immediately deported—end of discussion! As for the rest of them, any illegal immigrant that can prove he or she has been living here continuously for at least seven years, has not committed any crimes, has not been on the public dole, and has learned to speak English, should be allowed to stay and eventually get a work permit. However, they should receive no citizenship or "pathway to citizenship" and if they commit a future crime then their legal status should be revoked and they should be deported immediately. As for those who have been here for less than seven years, most of them should be tracked down, rounded up, and swiftly deported. However, we should not deport the elderly, the sick, or the disabled. We should also not deport orphans and widows.

Why not orphans and widows? Well, quite simply because scripture says that God doesn't look too favorably upon those who harden their hearts to the plight of orphans and widows. This is certainly not a perfect solution but perhaps it represents a fair and just middle-ground and one that is in keeping with the Judeo-Christian heritage that our nation was founded upon.

10

INSIST THAT NEW IMMIGRANTS FULLY ASSIMILATE

America used to be called a "melting-pot." Now we are just a tossed-salad. In the old days new immigrants were actually expected to assimilate and, indeed, they *wanted* to assimilate. When my ancestors came over from Russia they wanted to learn English, to learn about American history, and to become American citizens as soon as possible. They actually loved this country and were extremely grateful to be here. Nowadays that has all changed. Many immigrants who come here have more loyalty to their countries of origin than to the good old U.S. of A. Many of them care more about preserving their own languages and cultures than about learning English and assimilating into American culture. They are aided and abetted by liberals who are fanatical adherents to the new cult of "diversity" and "multiculturalism." This new cult decrees that it's more important for immigrants to maintain their own distinct languages and cultures than to learn English and assimilate into American culture. The liberals and multiculturalists believe it is downright racist and xenophobic for Americans to insist that new immigrants assimilate into American society.

To be clear, there are many immigrants who come here and who do wish to learn English and who do wish to assimilate. They love America and they're proud of their adopted home. Indeed, they're patriots and they should be welcomed with open arms. But as to the rest of them, especially the ingrates, a law should be passed that all immigrants must fully assimilate within a certain number of years. We should demand that their first and foremost loyalty be to the United States of America. While we are a nation of immigrants and should always be proud of our various cultures, this only goes so far. We ought to insist that new immigrants consider themselves to be Americans *first*. If placing America first is too much to ask then perhaps they should not have come here in the first place!

New immigrants should be expected to learn English. They should also be expected to learn about our history, our laws, and our culture. This isn't asking too much. In fact it's only asking the same thing that was asked of my ancestors and countless others who came to America in search of a better life. For all the great benefits and opportunities America gives to these immigrants, you would think that a little bit of gratitude and loyalty is not too much to expect! Any immigrants who refuse to meet these basic assimilation requirements should be denied citizenship and ultimately sent packing.

11

REDUCE LEGAL IMMIGRATION TO NOT MORE THAN 500,000 PER YEAR AND ELIMINATE "CHAIN MIGRATION"

America now has a population of well over 320 million and counting. We allow more legal immigration than any country in the world—over 1 million new legal immigrants each year. While we should always remain a beacon of light and hope to immigrants, we must also put our own national interests first. Yes, we are a nation of immigrants and we should continue to be a nation of immigrants but everything must have limits. We can't even properly assimilate all the immigrants that are already here. Many of them can't speak English and don't know a darn thing about our history, laws, or culture. A law should be passed that strictly limits the total number of legal immigrants to not more than 500,000 per year. This reduction will give us a chance to absorb and assimilate the millions of new immigrants that are already here.

Another way to reduce legal immigration is to get rid of "chain-migration." Just because a person comes to this country does not mean we should allow him to bring his whole extended family along too. Chain-migration should be strictly limited to immediate family members such as spouses and children.

12

DECLARE ENGLISH AS OUR OFFICIAL LANGUAGE

There is a story told in the Book of Genesis. It says that the people of the Earth were all of one language and they decided to build a tower all the way up to heaven—the Tower of Babel. As the story goes, God knew that because they were connected by a unified language they would be able to accomplish anything. So God decided that He would have to confuse their language before they became too powerful. It's a story children might read about in Sunday school but there is an important lesson to be learned. Language has great power. It has the power to create and the power to destroy. If people are not united by a common language they become weak and eventually will scatter into separate groups. Did you know that in the State of California you can now take your driver's license exam in not less than 31 different languages? And of course we've all heard the ubiquitous "press 1 for English" just about every time we make a call.

"A house divided against itself cannot stand." So said President Abraham Lincoln in 1858 when discussing why a nation can't survive half free and half slave. Lincoln's words apply to our times as well for we are fast becoming a house divided. First, we must understand one simple and irrefutable fact: Language is a powerful force that unites people together. Without a common language, a nation is not a nation. It is just a bunch of people living on the same plot of land. English was and is the national language of the United States but the multiculturalists aren't happy about that. Their goal is to remove English as our common language. Should they succeed, our "house," as Lincoln referred to it, will not stand. Make no mistake, the destruction of our common national language is a threat to the very survival our America as we know it.

President Theodore Roosevelt once said that "America has room for but one language—the English language." It's unbelievable that we've gotten to a point where we actually need to pass a law declaring English as America's national language. In a sane world there would be no need to pass such a law in the first place! But liberals have led a concerted effort to see to it that our common national language—the *English* language—is destroyed. No other country in the history of the world has voluntarily replaced its national language unless it was invaded and forced to do so. The multiculturalists and liberals say it's racist for us to insist on English as our national language. This notion is so absurd it hardly needs to be dignified with a response. Is France racist for speaking French? Is China racist for speaking Chinese? Is Spain racist for speaking Spanish? Why is it that all other nations have a right to a common national language but for some reason—at least in the minds of many liberals—America does not? English has been our common national language since this nation came into existence in 1776 and it was the common language of the original 13 colonies long before that.

A common language is part of the glue that binds a country together. In Federalist No. 2, John Jay mentions a common language as one of the things he is thankful for since it will help bind this nation together. Everyone seems to realize this except the liberals and multiculturalists who seem determined to have Spanish introduced as a national language co-equal with English. The fact that English is, and always has been, our common national language ought to be obvious. Thankfully, many states have already legally declared English as their official language, but that's not good enough.

A federal law needs to be passed that once and for all firmly and emphatically declares English to be America's national language. As part of this law all federal documents should be printed in English only and all federal websites should be in English only. States should also be required to put their documents and websites in English only, otherwise federal funds for state programs that don't comply should be cut off. Last but not least, all new immigrants should be legally required to learn English within a reasonable amount of time.

13

GET RID OF DUAL CITIZENSHIP

It's about time we get rid of people with divided loyalties. A nation needs citizens that are loyal and for too long liberals and multiculturalists have encouraged immigrants to have divided loyalties. This writer happens to be a Jew and feels a tremendous amount of love and affection towards the State of Israel; however, at the end of the day, I'm an *American* and my first loyalty is to the United States of America. It's time that we insist on loyalty from all our citizens. If you feel more loyalty towards Israel then you should live in Israel! If you are more loyal to Mexico then live in Mexico! It doesn't matter what country you come from, but if you move to the United States we have a right to expect your undivided loyalty.

A law should be passed that prohibits dual citizenship. Any immigrant who wishes to become an American citizen should first be required to formally and legally renounce any prior citizenship. In addition, absent extenuating circumstances, any American who becomes a citizen of a foreign country and/or serves in a foreign military should probably be stripped of his American citizenship.

14

PROMOTE AMERICANISM INSTEAD OF MULTICULTURALISM

Teddy Roosevelt once said, "We have room for but one flag, the American flag." The missionaries of multiculturalism spit upon that kind of sentiment and they detest Teddy Roosevelt. Liberals now have this new religion they call "multiculturalism." It declares all cultures to be equal and that American culture is in no way better than any other. Multiculturalists declare that the American flag, the English language, American history, American values, and American culture are not exceptional in any way. We shouldn't value our American culture any more than we value other cultures, they declare. To be clear, there is certainly nothing wrong with being proud of one's ancestry and wanting to preserve it. There is nothing wrong with a Jew being proud to be Jewish and cherishing his Jewish heritage. The same goes for one of Chinese, Greek, Mexican, or any other ancestry. We should all be proud of who we are and where we came from. We should embrace our heritage. But at the end of the day we must all be Americans *first*.

These demagogues of diversity, these missionaries of multiculturalism all seek to destroy the very heart of what it means to be an American. An American is one who bears full faith and allegiance to the Constitution of the United States, to our flag, to our history, and to our core values. The multiculturalists are not interested in any of that. They don't want us to be overly patriotic and they would rather people have more of a connection to their own religions, ethnic groups, and nations of origin than to the United States of America. Just being a patriotic American isn't good enough for them. They tell us we must instead be hyphenated-Americans. Just what is a hyphenated-American? Well, Teddy Roosevelt once declared that a hyphenated-American wasn't an American at all. Perhaps that goes a bit too far but at the very least a hyphenated-American is an American with divided loyalties.

Make no mistake about it, this new emphasis on multiculturalism and hyphenated-Americanism is a recipe for disaster. A country must be united in order to survive and thrive. To be united, a country must have a common culture and citizens that are proud of that culture. Let's be perfectly clear, this new religion—this cult—of multiculturalism will be the ruination of America. We are fast becoming the "polyglot boarding house" that Teddy Roosevelt warned us about. We must heed his warning before it's too late: "The one absolutely certain way of bringing this nation to ruin, of preventing all possibility of its continuing to be a nation at all, would be to permit it to become a tangle of squabbling nationalities," said Roosevelt.

How do we solve this problem? States should pass "Americanism" laws in education. Instead of indoctrinating students into the new religion of multiculturalism and instead of spending $25,000 dollars in taxpayer money to install footbaths for Muslims at the University of Michigan, students should be taught the value and importance of our unique *American* culture. They should be taught to be proud of our flag, our language, our laws, our history, and, in a word, our culture.

15

PUT UNITY BEFORE DIVERSITY

Liberals are simply obsessed with the concept of "diversity." Their new religion of "diversity" is closely associated with their love of multiculturalism. All of this has to stop. We need to put unity before diversity. The name of this country is the *United* States of America, not the Diverse States of America! If one reads the Declaration of Independence, the Constitution, the Federalist Papers, the Gettysburg Address, or just about any of our nation's most essential documents, how many times will he find the importance of racial, ethnic, or religious diversity mentioned? The answer is zero. This nation was not built by obsessing over diversity, rather, we became great by our unity, by uniting people from various backgrounds to become one people—the *American* people. There is certainly nothing wrong with diversity in itself. As a matter of fact, being exposed to people of diverse backgrounds is generally a very good thing. But the liberals have taken it to extreme proportions. They are utterly fixated upon diversity. You may have heard of OCD—Obsessive Compulsive Disorder. Well, most liberals suffer from OCDD—Obsessive Compulsive Diversity Disorder. Enough is enough. We must put a stop to this craziness. If we are to save America then we must stop this insanity and start focusing more on unity and less on diversity. We must have a truly *United* States of America—not a Divided States of America.

16

EMBRACE THE IDEA OF AMERICAN EXCEPTIONALISM ONCE AGAIN

Remember Superman? He fought for "truth, justice, and the American way." Yes, the *American* way. Nowadays liberals would call Superman jingoistic, xenophobic, divisive, and maybe even racist. This country used to embrace the idea of "American exceptionalism." Just what is American exceptionalism? What is this idea that is so odious to most of our friends on the Left? American exceptionalism is the idea that America is unique, that we are different from most other countries, that we are, in a word, exceptional. Nowadays liberals cringe at this idea. They claim that America is no better than any other country. How dare we think ourselves exceptional?

If we are to save America we must once again embrace the idea of American exceptionalism. Let the liberals call us jingoistic, ethnocentric, and divisive. Who cares? We must embrace once again the notion that America *is* the greatest nation on God's green earth and that we really *are* that "shining city on a hill." Sure, we make mistakes—sometimes very great mistakes. And no, we most certainly aren't perfect and have plenty of things we ought to regret. But on the whole, we have been the greatest experiment in human liberty this world has ever known! We have done more to advance the cause of freedom than just about any other nation on this planet. We have twice saved Western civilization; once from Nazism and once from totalitarian Marxism. Without America, where would the world be? For all of our very real faults, the world still needs America. The world still needs an America that is proud and strong and knows what she is capable of. So let's stop putting ourselves down and let's embrace "truth, justice, and the American way" once again!

17

CELEBRATE THE ACHIEVEMENTS OF WESTERN CIVILIZATION

The demagogues of diversity and the missionaries of multiculturalism tell us that all cultures are the same. We can't dare to say that any civilization or culture is superior to any other, for that would be divisive, offensive, jingoistic, and maybe even racist. Most of all, we can't dare to say or even think that Western civilization might be superior to any other. However, truth be told, Western civilization *is* superior to other civilizations! To be very clear, this does not mean that other cultures and civilizations are not valuable and important—they are. It does not mean we should degrade or disparage the many important contributions from non-Western cultures—we shouldn't. All civilizations and cultures have great value and add delicious flavors to this wonderful world of ours. On the other hand, we don't need to pretend that all cultures and civilizations are inherently equal—they aren't.

Timothy M. Rosen

Western civilization has contributed more to this world than just about any other. The following is just a small sample: The idea of basic human rights and individual liberty came from the West. Things like the freedom of speech, freedom of religion, a free press, and freedom of assembly, these all came from Western civilization. Due process of law, the right to a speedy and fair trial, the right to be secure in one's home against unreasonable searches, the right to counsel, and the notion of equality before the law, these too are all the product of Western civilization. The great Writ of Habeas Corpus also originated in the West. Democracy, women's suffrage, civil rights— these too originated in the West. The English common law, by far the most influential legal system in the world today, is also a product of Western civilization.

The list goes on. The Enlightenment originated in the West. Many of the world's greatest philosophers and theologians have come from the West. The overwhelming majority of Nobel Prize winners have been from the West. The vast majority of the world's greatest inventions such as the steam engine, the locomotive, the airplane, the automobile, the television, antibiotics, the telephone, and even air conditioning are all products of Western civilization. So while it's certainly true that all cultures and civilizations have value, and while all have made important contributions to the world in one way or another, none of them have had the monumental impact that Western civilization has had on this world. We should be proud of that.

It's nothing to be ashamed of! We should not hide from our accomplishments. It's time to once again embrace the exceptional nature of Western civilization.

18

TEACH KIDS TO RESPECT AMERICA'S FOUNDING FATHERS

George Washington used to be thought of as a hero, as the "Father of our Country." School kids used to be taught to respect America's Founding Fathers. Sadly, this is no longer the case in many parts of the country. Some school districts have even changed the names of schools that once honored America's Founding Fathers. If we are to save America we must stop allowing liberals to indoctrinate young people with their hatred of the Founding Fathers. A nation's culture can't long endure when its national heroes are besmirched and its children taught to hate them. Were the Founding Fathers perfect men? No, certainly not. They were human beings and as such they were highly imperfect men who made their share of mistakes. Nonetheless they were still great men. If it were not for their wisdom and their sacrifice there would be no America today. Of this there can be no doubt.

Yes, a few of them were slaveholders and that is an indelible stain upon their memory; however, that does not invalidate the great accomplishments of these men. Those who were slaveholders probably knew the evil nature of slavery but they were a product of their times. We ought not to excuse or condone the sheer evil that was slavery in America; however, we must also realize that slavery existed all over the world and in just about every culture since the dawn of civilization. It was simply a fact of life on this planet. It should also be emphasized that not all of the Founding Fathers were slaveholders. Some were and others were not. John Adams utterly abhorred slavery. George Washington did own slaves but saw to it in his will that all of his slaves would eventually be emancipated. Thomas Jefferson, reflecting upon the institution of slavery—an institution he was very much responsible for—said, "Indeed, I tremble for my country when I reflect that God is just: that His justice cannot sleep forever."

For all their very human faults, the Founding Fathers were still great men and but for their wisdom, courage, and tenacity, there would be no America. In order to save America we must save our culture and it can't be denied that the Founding Fathers have played a major role in shaping this nation's history and culture. It's time to once again teach kids to admire and respect our Founding Fathers!

19

TEACH MORALS INSTEAD
OF MORAL RELATIVISM

We used to teach kids the difference between right and wrong. Right was right and wrong was wrong. Not so anymore. It seems that the idea of morals is now obsolete, replaced by moral relativism. Be it profanity or promiscuity, pretty much anything goes. If it feels good, just do it. There is no right and wrong anymore. There are just feelings. Above all else, just remember one thing: Don't be even the slightest bit judgmental! That is the worst sin of all, they tell us. We can't dare to judge anyone else's morals for all of our morals are equal and none is better than the other.

Perhaps it's time we stop indoctrinating young people into this cult of moral relativism and start teaching them about morals once again. Perhaps it's about time we get rid of all this moral relativism and return to our Judeo-Christian roots. Many of those on the Left, particularly atheists for whom moral relativism is a core belief, will find this appalling. Atheists might be enamored with moral relativism but it was not atheists that built this country. In order to save America we must once again instill a sense of morality into our citizens. It was John Adams who said, "Our Constitution was made only for a moral and religious people." And it was George Washington who once said, "Of all the dispositions and habits which lead to political prosperity, religion and morality are indispensable supports."

20

MERIT PAY FOR TEACHERS

The teachers unions loathe the idea of merit pay. For them merit pay is a heretical concept. Oh sure, the teachers unions tell us that they really care about the kids and want the best for them. Don't believe it. There are most certainly many wonderful teachers who truly care about their students but the teachers unions are a different story. They care more about themselves than they do about the success of students. Why is it that in the private sector merit pay is commonplace? If an employee in the private sector has a really good year and he or she makes a lot of sales or shows herself to be particularly efficient and effective, she will most likely get a bonus or a raise in salary. This is just common sense. We reward people who deserve it. Someone who works harder and does a better job deserves to be rewarded for that. The teachers unions don't want any part of that. They want all teachers to be paid exactly the same no matter how terrible or how wonderful

a teacher might be. If you have one teacher who is working her tail off to make sure all her students do well and
another teacher who doesn't really care and is ineffective
and lazy, the teachers unions want them both to make the
exact same amount of money. This is totally illogical and
it is undermining America's educational system as we are
falling further and further behind other countries. If we
are to save America we must save our schools. We must
fix and reinvigorate our whole educational system and a
good way to start is with merit pay for all teachers.

21

ELIMINATE TEACHER TENURE

This is another idea that the teachers unions hate. It's similar to the idea of merit pay but should be even more of a "no-brainer." Why on earth should a teacher get a lifetime job appointment? How does that make them a better teacher? In fact, it's just the opposite. Once teachers get tenure they have virtually lifetime job security and so they're more likely to be lazy, complacent, and will have less incentive to work hard and get results. To be clear, there are certainly some terrific teachers out there who would continue to work hard whether or not they have tenure but for most that's not the case. It's just basic human nature. Why should a person work extra hard if he doesn't have to? If a teacher has a lifetime job contract and it's not dependent upon his or her job performance, what motivation is there to work harder and become a better teacher? The very idea of tenure for teachers is absurd and it should be totally done away with. It doesn't even exist in the private sector at all. In the private sector there is no such thing as lifetime job security that is not tied to one's job performance. For instance, if a baseball player is hired he is expected to hit home runs and help his team win championships. If he does so his contract will get renewed and he will get more money. If not, he might not keep his job at all. It's basic common sense. There must be a sufficient financial motivation for a person to work hard. Teacher tenure does absolutely nothing to motivate teachers to work harder or perform better. It does just the opposite—it promotes laziness and complacency.

Tenure is also unfair for another reason. Many teachers unions insist on a "last in first out" rule. This means that if there are budget cuts and teachers have to be laid off, the teachers who have been there the longest will probably keep their jobs—no matter how good or bad of a teacher they might be. A new teacher who is phenomenal at his or her job will nonetheless be the first to go. What needs to go is the whole system of teacher tenure. It's helping to ruin our educational system as America falls further and further behind other countries. Instead of tenure, teachers should get a contract for a set period of time. At the end of their contract term there should be a full and fair review. If they have been efficient and done a great job then their contract should be renewed and they should be rewarded with a substantial pay raise. On the other hand, if their students have been failing then the teacher should be put on probation. If the teacher improves at his or her job during this probationary period then they should be able to continue as a teacher. However, if they don't improve then we should put the kids first and fire bad teachers!

22

PAY TEACHERS MORE AND ADMINISTRATORS LESS

Our nation's teachers perform one of the most important jobs there is—educating America's children. There are few jobs more vital. We need the best and the brightest people out there to become teachers and the only way to get the best and the brightest is to pay them what they are worth. We pay grown men millions of dollars to throw a ball around, the least we can do is pay our teachers what they deserve. If we are to save America we must save our deteriorating educational system. How do we do this? Get rid of the education bureaucrats. Cut their bloated salaries and instead start paying teachers what they truly deserve. Teachers should get a very lucrative base salary but this must be increased or decreased based directly upon their performance—i.e. merit pay.

The starting salary for a teacher should be not less than $65,000 dollars per year and it should not be unheard of for outstanding educators to earn upwards of $140,000 per year or even more—so long as their pay is strictly tied to the success of their students. Meanwhile, the bloated educational bureaucracy needs to be cut. A lot of these education bureaucrats need to find another line of work completely and the ones that remain need to have their bloated salaries cut. In no event should any school administrator earn more than our highest paid teachers. America needs better teachers, not better bureaucrats!

23

STOP THE LEFT-WING INDOCTRINATION OF AMERICA'S SCHOOLCHILDREN

*"Children should be educated and in-
structed in the principles of freedom."*

—JOHN ADAMS

Laws must be passed in every state to prohibit the Leftist indoctrination of schoolchildren. The federal government should also cut off federal funds to any school district that that engages in left-wing indoctrination. Is such indoctrination really a big problem? Here are but a few examples:

- Students at a California school were sent home for wearing t-shirts emblazoned with the American flag because it might offend Mexican students

- The Seattle public schools have used Thanksgiving as a chance to bash America and tell students how it's a "day of mourning" for Native Americans
- California has passed a law requiring that students be taught about the historical contributions of lesbian, gay, bisexual, and transgender Americans.
- Students in McAllen, Texas were forced to memorize and recite the Mexican national anthem and pledge of allegiance.
- Students in New York City middle and high schools are required to take graphic sexual education classes that include a lesson on how to properly use condoms. Parents are not even allowed to opt out.

If we are to save America this has to stop. Schools should focus on reading, writing, and arithmetic—not on how to use condoms, not on memorizing the Mexican national anthem, and not on teaching kids to hate Thanksgiving! Any teacher that indoctrinates students with anti-American hatred should be fired. Any school district that condones or encourages it should lose all federal funds. History teachers ought to be honest and objective and should not use their classrooms as a platform to bash America. Under no circumstances should students be taught to despise our history, our laws, our culture, or our Founding Fathers.

24

ELIMINATE SOCIAL PROMOTION AND INSIST ON HIGH STANDARDS IN EDUCATION

America must once again insist on the highest standards in education. Students who can't read or write at grade level should not be promoted on to the next grade—no exceptions. A high school diploma should actually mean something instead of being just a worthless piece of paper. Not only must we eliminate social promotion but we must hold the schools accountable. If kids are failing to learn then their teachers and school administrators should be held accountable—in their pocketbooks. Failing schools should be shut down, failing administrators and failing teachers should be fired, and failing students should be given all the help they need to succeed.

25

INSIST UPON INTELLECTUAL DIVERSITY AMONGST UNIVERSITY FACULTY

Liberal indoctrination is not just a problem in middle school and high school. It's also happening—and is much more severe—on most college campuses. The fact is most college students only get to hear one side of things—the Leftist side. That's because liberal professors greatly out-number conservative professors on your typical college campus. A 2012 study out of UCLA found that 50.3% of professors identify as liberal and an additional 12.4% iden-tify as "far left." That's a total of almost 63% of professors who identify as liberal or "far left." Meanwhile, less than 12% of professors identify as conservative or "far right."

Many of these professors are not just liberals but outright Marxists who indoctrinate students to hate tra-ditional American values. The irony in all this is that liber-als in academia claim to love diversity. They insist upon diversity when it comes to race, religion, gender, and sexual orientation but they don't seem to care very much about another kind of diversity—intellectual diversity. They are happy to have students brainwashed with their views and not exposed to conservative ideas. This liberal brainwashing of college students must stop. If the liberals love diversity so much then we should insist that they also promote more intellectual diversity on campus. College students deserve to hear both sides of things and to then make up their own minds.

26

FIRE COLLEGE PROFESSORS WHO ATTEMPT TO INDOCTRINATE THEIR STUDENTS OR VIOLATE ACADEMIC FREEDOM

College professors are supposed to respect the academic freedom of their students and aren't supposed to use their classrooms as their own personal soapboxes. They're also supposed to develop the critical thinking skills of their students by exposing them to a multitude of ideas. College is supposed to a place where the free and fair exchange of ideas is not only allowed but encouraged. Unfortunately, what college professors are *supposed* to do and what they *actually* do are often two different things. As someone who spent four years as a college student and has spent an additional seven years as a college professor, this writer can attest to the fact that liberal indoctrination is alive and well on campus.

To save America we must put a stop to the ongoing left-wing indoctrination of college students. A country can't long survive if future leaders are being brainwashed to hate its economic system, its values, its history, and its heroes. At the very least, it's time that professors are held to their own professional standards. According to the American Association of University Professors (the AAUP), as promulgated in the Statement of Principles on Academic Freedom and Tenure, college professors are to be careful not to introduce controversial subject-matter that is not relevant to their course. A literature professor, for instance, should not be spending class time denouncing capitalism and lambasting the Republican Party.

More importantly, professors are required to protect the academic freedom of their students and to encourage the free exchange of ideas. According to the AAUP's Joint Statement on Rights and Freedoms of Students, "The professor in the classroom and in conference should encourage free discussion, inquiry, and expression. Student performance should be evaluated solely on an academic basis, not on opinions or conduct in matters unrelated to academic standards...Students should be free to take reasoned exception to the data or views offered in any course of study and to reserve judgment about matters of opinion, but they are responsible for learning the content of any course of study for which they are enrolled."

Professors should be given a clear choice: Either abide by your own professional standards of conduct or find another line of work! A federal law must be passed that cuts off any and all federal funds to any college that does not take concrete steps to protect the academic freedom of students from liberal professors run amuck.

27

MAKE COLLEGE MORE AFFORDABLE

*"Freedom can exist only in the society
of knowledge."*

—BENJAMIN RUSH

Millions of students are now being crushed under a mountain of debt just because they want a college education. In an enlightened society every citizen should be able to get a good education without going into debt that will last a lifetime. Moreover, a country needs to have a well-educated citizenry. It's simply good public policy to see to it that our citizens can get a good education without going bankrupt. In the past many public universities used to be tuition-free. We need to find a way to get back to that. That should really be the goal—public universities that offer our citizens free education. Of course, it's not really free at all since our tax dollars already go to pay for these universities! Another way to cut the costs of a college education is to cut the salaries of the educational bureaucrats. Cut their fat and bloated salaries and use the savings to make college more affordable for all.

28

REPUDIATE THE RACE-BAITERS

Some people's words and actions have done great harm to our country. Al Sharpton is one such person. How it is that Al Sharpton ever came to be regarded as an authority on race is beyond comprehension. The man is himself a racist and, even worse, he has blood on his hands. In 1991, during the Crown Heights Riots, he helped to incite anti-Semitic violence. In 1995 he called a Jewish landlord in Harlem a "white interloper." His racial incitement that year ended with innocent people being murdered when Freddy's Fashion Mart was fire bombed. He has also been caught on tape using all sorts of racial and anti-gay epithets. And yet, inexplicably, Sharpton has been embraced by the liberal media and the Democratic Party. They should all be ashamed of themselves.

As bad as Sharpton is, he is merely a symptom of a larger problem. Whether it's Al Sharpton screaming about "white interlopers" or liberal professors like Michael Eric

Dyson ranting about "white privilege," this type of attitude is destructive to the unity of our country. We need to come together as one nation—a nation united, not divided. How can America ever come together with race-baiters like Sharpton constantly running around stirring up racial animus?

No intelligent person denies that America has a very troubled history when it comes to race. The enslavement of millions of Africans was utterly evil and is a stain on our history. However, slavery has been gone for 150 years! We now have had numerous blacks in congress, we've had black cabinet secretaries, black generals, black mayors, black governors, black justices of the Supreme Court, and of course, a black president. Listening to the race-baiters one would get the impression that blacks were still picking cotton and Rosa Parks was still standing in the back of the bus. They act as though nothing has changed in 150 years. They insist that white people must walk with perpetual guilt for the actions of the distant past. They believe that when it comes to racism (which they see lurking around every corner) white people are guilty until proven innocent. They constantly seek to stir up racial tensions and divisions. They literally make a fortune on race-baiting, for them it is a career and a very lucrative one at that.

In order to save America we have to somehow put a stop to all this race-baiting. People like Al Sharpton should be shunned by society. Race-baiters should be told to find another line of work. We must rid ourselves of this unhealthy national obsession with race but it's hard to do that with race-baiting charlatans like Al Sharpton running amuck. In order to save America we must be *one* America. There is no black America. There is no white America. There is just America. We are not black Americans. We are not white Americans. We are just Americans. That is something the race-baiters will never understand.

29

GET RID OF AFFIRMATIVE ACTION

Affirmative action was started by good people with good intentions. They meant well. They felt it was necessary to fix the wrongs of the past. But the fact remains that affirmative action has not helped minorities—it has hurt them. Unemployment and poverty are no less of a problem in the black community today than before affirmative action came along. Worse yet, affirmative action tells blacks and other "underrepresented minorities" that they are inferior, that they can't make it on their own. They're told they need the government to step in and give them a hand, that otherwise they just won't be able to be successful on their own. This seems pretty insulting. Clarence Thomas, the second black man to sit upon the U.S. Supreme Court, wrote the following about his time as a student at Yale: "…affirmative action (though it wasn't yet called that) had become a fact of life at American colleges and universities, and before long I realized that those blacks who benefited from it were being judged by a double standard. As much as it stung to be told that I'd done well in seminary despite my race, it was far worse to feel that I was now at Yale because of it."

Affirmative action today goes far beyond the idea of correcting past discrimination. Liberals today are absolutely *obsessed* with the idea of promoting "diversity." Diversity has become almost a cult-like religion amongst them. They view anything and everything through this prism of diversity. This obsession with diversity is linked to their fanatical obsession with race. They view everything in terms of race and want racial diversity to be priority number one. They believe diversity to be so important that colleges, employers, graduate schools, and the government have a sacred duty to promote it at all costs— even if that means lowering standards or violating the equal rights of others. This is not only unfair but absurd. Why is promoting "diversity" more important than promoting high standards and advancement based on merit? Should the liberal quest for perfect diversity trump everything else?

Were we not taught that "two wrongs don't make a right." Is it right to discriminate against white males because other groups have suffered from racism and discrimination? Even if affirmative action worked—which it doesn't—how can this sort of reverse discrimination ever be justified? Do the ends justify the means? The Rev. Dr. Martin Luther King Jr. dreamed of a day when people would be judged "not by the color of their skin but by the content of their character." As long as America clings to affirmative action and this fanatical obsession with diversity and race, Rev. King's dream will remain just that—a dream.

30

SIMPLIFY THE TAX CODE—GET RID OF ALL THE LOOPHOLES

The Internal Revenue Code is thousands of pages long, filled with incomprehensible rules and regulations that only the most highly trained tax lawyer can hope to understand. It's also filled with loopholes that allow wealthy individuals and powerful corporations to weasel their way out of paying their share. The average Joe can't afford to hire a team of tax lawyers and accountants to comb through the tax code and pick out all the best loopholes. It's time we put a stop to this unfairness. Wealthy individuals and corporations should have to pay their fair share and not hide behind these loopholes. The entire tax code needs to be totally overhauled and we must totally eliminate all the loopholes. The tax code should be simple and easy to read and should take up no more than a few pages of paper.

31

ESTABLISH A MORE PROGRESSIVE INCOME TAX BUT WITH A TOP RATE OF NOT MORE THAN 30%

Many libertarians think we shouldn't even have a federal income tax to begin with. However, if we are going to have a federal income tax at all then it should be progressive. While many fiscal conservatives favor a flat-tax, a progressive income tax is the most fair. A 15% tax on someone only earning 30,000 dollars per year is a lot more onerous than the same 15% tax on someone earning 300,000 dollars per year. While it is true that we already have a progressive income tax, it should be made even more progressive and all the loopholes should be eliminated. The top tax rate, however, should be no higher than 30%. Why 30%? All Americans—both rich and poor alike—deserve to keep the vast majority of what they earn through their own hard work. Americans at every income level are currently being over-taxed and they deserve to keep more of their hard-earned money in their own pockets. Therefore, the tax code should be completely overhauled and simplified.

First off, no more loopholes—everyone pays their fair share. Here is a suggestion as to a possible tax rate. This is just a general suggestion and the numbers can certainly be debated.

- Income under 25,000 dollars should be taxed at 2%
- income between 25,000 dollars and 50,000 dollars should be taxed at 10%
- income between 50,000 dollars and 100,000 dollars should be taxed at 15%
- income between 100,000 dollars and 200,000 dollars should be taxed at 20%
- income between 200,000 dollars and 500,000 dollars should be taxed at 25%
- income between 500,000 dollars and 1,000,000 dollars should be taxed at 28%
- income over 1,000,000 dollars should be taxed at 30%

Again, these are just some general suggestions and the numbers are not set in stone. The basic idea, however, is that we need a clear, easy to understand tax code, a tax code without loopholes for the wealthy, and a tax code that allows all people of all income levels to keep the vast majority of what they earn.

32

ELIMINATE ALL FORMS OF CORPORATE WELFARE—NO MORE CRONY CAPITALISM!

One often hears complaints about poor people getting "handouts" from the government. But why is it somehow ok for the wealthy to get government handouts? If a billionaire real-estate developer wishes to put up a new shopping mall or something like that, let him use his own damn money to do it! And if a big corporation is about to go under, why should the taxpayers bail it out as we did during the financial crisis of 2008-2009? Do we believe in the free-market or not? If we do then it's high time we eliminate all forms of corporate welfare once and for all— no more myriad tax loopholes, no more sweetheart deals, no more bailouts, no more crony capitalism!

33

PASS A BALANCED BUDGET AMENDMENT TO THE CONSTITUTION

"A public debt is a public curse."

-JAMES MADISON

If James Madison knew the extent of our national debt to-day he would likely be dumbfounded. Let's be very clear. Our national debt will eventually destroy the United States of America as we know it. It's so enormous as to be almost beyond human comprehension. Our current national debt is over 19 trillion dollars and counting. This crushing level of debt is simply not sustainable and will eventually bring our country to ruin. We simply can't continue to spend more money than we take it. It's a mathematical reality. And by the way, this 19 trillion dollar debt does not even include the tens of trillions of dollars in unfunded liabilities for entitlements such as Social Security.

Who is to blame for this crushing national debt? The Republicans? The Democrats? The fact is they are both to blame! This stupendous level of debt has been the work of both Republican and Democratic administrations over the course of decades. In more recent years, however, the pace has picked up dramatically. When Bill Clinton left office in January 2001, he left us with a debt of about 5.5 trillion dollars. George W. Bush came along and in his two terms doubled our debt. Bush added more to our debt than any other president in American history—that is until Barack Obama came along. During Obama's tenure we have seen our national debt skyrocket even faster than under Bush. It should also be noted that the U.S. Congress shares a lot of the blame as well. It is Congress that controls the "power of the purse." Members of Congress from both political parties have helped to get us into this mess.

The bottom line is that politicians in both political parties are spending our money like the proverbial drunken sailor and their profligate ways will lead America to ruin. Neither party can be trusted. That is why we need to pass a balanced budget amendment to the Constitution. The proposed amendment would be very simple: At the end of each fiscal year the budget of the federal government will be balanced. The federal government shall be prohibited from spending more money than it takes in and no debt shall be incurred. The only exception shall be in a time of war or national emergency when the Congress may, by a 2/3 vote, temporarily allow the government to run a deficit and incur debt. Save America! Pass a balanced budget amendment now!

34

GET RID OF THE NORTH AMERICAN FREE TRADE AGREEMENT—NAFTA

NAFTA—the North American Free Trade Agreement—was supposed to be a great benefit to the American economy. When it was passed over 20 years ago it was hailed by members of both political parties. What have been the fruits of NAFTA and similar free-trade agreements? What has this free-trade fanaticism done for America? Has it helped the average American worker? Has it helped our economy? Has it lowered our national debt? The answer is no. None of these things happened. NAFTA supporters predicted that it would be great for our economy and that we would enjoy a large trade surplus with Mexico. Instead, just the opposite happened. In the three years prior to NAFTA taking effect, the U.S. actually had a trade surplus with Mexico. Ever since NAFTA our trade surplus with Mexico has completely vanished and we have had trade deficits with Mexico every year. The average American worker has also suffered as corporations have outsourced jobs to Mexico and other countries. It's time to rethink NAFTA and all of these other "free trade" agreements. It's time to get rid of all this free-trade fanaticism and to start protecting the American worker once again.

35

BRING BACK "MADE IN THE USA"

Over the last 20 years or so America has been led down the path of free-trade fanaticism. Free-trade agreements like NAFTA have hurt the American worker and have made it easier for corporations to outsource jobs to other countries. We have lost millions of our manufacturing jobs to countries like China and Mexico. When was the last time you purchased something that was "Made in the USA"? In the decade between 2000 and 2010 America lost 33% of her manufacturing jobs—5.7 million American jobs gone. Our trade deficits have become larger and our manufacturing jobs have become fewer. It's time for this to stop. As previously discussed, we ought to seriously rethink all of these free-trade agreements. Secondly, corporations that agree to keep their manufacturing plants in America and can proudly declare that all of their products are "Made in the USA," should be rewarded with substantial tax breaks.

36

SAVE SOCIAL SECURITY AND MEDICARE

Social Security and Medicare are both going bankrupt. These programs also substantially contribute to our federal budget deficits and our monumental national debt. In short, these entitlement programs are bankrupting the whole country. Nevertheless, these programs should be saved. They've benefited and continue to benefit tens of millions of our fellow citizens. How do we save them without bankrupting the country? It's quite simple and can be expressed in two words: means-testing. It's absolutely ludicrous that billionaires like Michael Bloomberg, Warren Buffet, and Donald Trump are all entitled to a Social Security check every month. Social Security and Medicare should be there for our seniors if they truly need it but there needs to be an income and net worth cut off for these programs. For example, let's say person retires at 65 with a pension and investment income in the amount of $100,000 per year. In that case, he or she does not need a social security check. Means -testing would save these programs for the people who truly need them and would also stop these programs from further bankrupting our country.

37

GET RID OF WELFARE AND
REPLACE IT WITH THE WPA

Sometimes people lose their jobs. Sometimes they fall on hard times. We are a generous and caring nation and we have an absolute moral obligation to provide help for such people. However, it seems that welfare is going about it the wrong way. It's rather degrading to give someone a handout when you could give them a job instead. Our welfare programs also create a cycle of dependency. Instead of offering a temporary hand, people are sucked into a cycle of poverty and government dependency that is hard to break. But there is a possible solution: Get rid of welfare and replace it with a new version of the WPA.

The WPA, the Works Progress Administration, was one of the largest and boldest of Franklin Roosevelt's New Deal programs. At its peak it provided jobs to millions of unemployed workers. Parks, bridges, roads, buildings, and all manner of infrastructure were built or repaired by the workers of the WPA. Instead of handing out welfare checks and thus creating a sense of dependency, it's time to reactivate the WPA. Many of America's roads and bridges are badly in need of repair. There and trees to plant, schools to build, bridges to maintain, airports to modernize, and solar panels to install. Heck, we could even put people to work building a 2,000 mile fence on the Mexican border to finally put a stop to illegal immigration! The point is that instead of giving out welfare we can take that same money and give people jobs while improving our infrastructure at the same time. Bring back the WPA!

38

RAISE THE MINIMUM WAGE

Many conservatives and libertarians don't like the idea of a minimum wage and would rather abolish it altogether. They take a strong and principled position that wages are best left to the free market to decide. Their position is quite reasonable and they may well have a valid point. However, many others believe that making sure workers, especially low-income workers, can put a roof over their heads and put food on the table is simply the right thing to do. The fact that a person can work very hard at a full-time job and yet still qualify for food stamps is outrageous. Moreover, having a living wage is simply good public policy and a society has a right to make laws that are in its best interests. Having millions of "working poor" who, despite working full-time jobs still can't pay the rent or put food on the table is bad for all of society. For instance, according to an article in Forbes, Walmart alone costs taxpayers $6.2 billion dollars per year in public assistance programs.

Is it fair for Walmart and other companies to make the American taxpayer pick up the slack because they won't pay their workers a living wage? Imagine the benefits to society if workers at Walmart and elsewhere were all making a good living. It should be noted that after years of public pressure and bad press, Walmart has recently agreed to raise the wages of their workers to at least $10 dollars an hour. It's about time!

What if other companies did the same? Millions of workers would not need to be on food stamps, welfare, or Medicaid. Imagine how much money would be saved by the American taxpayer. Even more importantly, imagine how much stronger and prosperous our economy would be if we once again had a strong and prosperous middle class. It is time to raise the federal minimum wage to at least $10 dollars an hour and to have automatic cost of living increases each year to keep pace with inflation. In addition, large cities such as New York and Chicago, where the cost of living is extremely high, should have an even higher minimum wage.

39

CREATE A WORKER'S "BILL OF RIGHTS"

Libertarians and economic conservatives will probably not like this idea one bit. Their position is consistent, reasonable, and principled; however, this writer must respectfully disagree. Apart from laws barring discrimination, America remains the only civilized nation in the world that does not provide basic rights for workers. Great Britain, France, Canada, Australia, etc., all provide their citizens with certain rights in the workplace. The average working Joe deserves a job that treats him fairly and humanely. Employers ought to treat employees the way they themselves would wish to be treated. Compared to most countries in the West, however, American workers enjoy very few benefits. If America is to be saved we must once again build up a strong and prosperous middle class. It's time to give the average worker more of a "square deal," as Teddy Roosevelt might say. To be clear, this new law would not apply to small businesses—the typical mom &

pop shop. It would only apply to companies that engage in interstate commerce and have 15 or more employees. At a bare minimum, this new worker's "Bill of Rights" should have the following components:

- All employees should receive at least 15 days paid vacation each year
- All employees should receive up to 30 days paid family and/or medical leave each year
- After working at a company for two years or more, an employee fired without cause should be entitled to at least six months of severance pay
- All employees should be provided with medical and dental insurance
- All employees should be provided with a reasonable pension

40

SAVE THE MIDDLE CLASS

Nowadays anyone who talks about income inequality is supposedly a Marxist. It may well be true that many of those who talk about income inequality have Marxist tendencies and so let's be crystal clear: If one believes in freedom then he must also believe in the free market. Freedom means being free to bring your goods to market. Freedom means being free to enter into private contracts with other free individuals. Freedom means being free to start your own business. In short, freedom and the free market are inextricably linked. In addition, free market capitalism has brought more prosperity to more people than any other economic system ever devised. Thus, the free market should be respected and admired for there is no better economic system known to man.

Nevertheless, no system is perfect and in the last 40 years or so the poor and the middle class have been falling further and further behind. Meanwhile, the wealthy have been getting further and further ahead. This is not meant to demonize wealth or wealthy people. We should want America to have lots and lots of very wealthy folks for they create jobs and economic prosperity. The problem is that the gap between the wealthy and the middle class has grown wider than it has ever been before and this is not healthy for our economy or for our country.

Now to be clear, unless you're a Marxist, you will accept the fact that there will always be a gap between rich and poor. But does that gap have to be the size of the Grand Canyon? Is that good for our nation? In a free society there will never be "income equality" but that doesn't mean we should turn a blind eye to the ever widening gap between rich and poor. Henry Ford understood that in order for his business to succeed and in order for him to make even more money, he needed to have workers that made enough money to buy his cars! Milton Hershey, the famous chocolatier, also understood that treating his workers well was both the right thing to do morally and the smart thing to do economically. He created an entire town, Hershey, Pennsylvania in which his factory workers owned their own homes, had fresh air and recreation, and earned a decent living. Henry Ford and Milton Hershey understood what too many corporate CEOs today have forgotten: Building up a strong middle class, with well paid workers, is not only the right thing to do, it's also good for business and thus good for America.

Starting in the late 1960s, the gap between the salaries of the average American worker and average American CEO has grown much wider. This is not good for workers, not good for business, and not good for America. In a country that respects the centrality of the free market (as we ought to) there is no quick fix for this problem but the first step is to recognize it and to begin to have a national conversation about it. There may be no quick fix or perfect solution to this problem but one thing is clear: If we are to save America we must have a strong and prosperous middle class.

41

HELP THE POOR

If we truly practice what we preach and we truly believe that America is a nation founded upon Judeo-Christian values, then we must surely do more to help not just the middle class but especially the poor. The Jewish and Christian scriptures both exhort us to take care of the poor numerous times. We can certainly argue about the best way to accomplish this and some would say that creating government dependency does more harm than good. Perhaps we've gone about it in the wrong way. In any event, however we accomplish it, as a nation a lot more needs to be done. Yes, we are a generous nation and yes we already do a lot. But that is just not good enough. A lot more needs to be done. Working to reduce poverty and to uplift the poor should be a national priority.

Perhaps it's because I grew up poor and because I know what poverty is, that I take a special interest in this issue. Poverty knows no race or creed. It can affect a white man in rural West Virginia, a Latino family in New York, or an Asian woman in California. Yes, it's certainly true that some people are poor because of their own poor choices; however, it is equally true that some people are poor because they simply can't make ends meet no matter how hard they try.

What can be done to ameliorate poverty? That's a good question and there is no easy answer. The first thing to do is for America to make the plight of the poor a priority once again. If we can spend—some would say waste—tens of billions of dollars on a "war on drugs" then we can and should do more to help pull people out of poverty. We should insist that the poor not be vilified and made into scapegoats but at the same time we should not create in them a mentality of perpetual victimhood and entitlement. Before handing out a welfare check we should first see if we can hand someone a paycheck. There should of course be a strong social safety net but instead of just giving people handouts we should give them a "hand up." Better education, job training, more affordable housing, a new WPA, and a higher minimum wage might be a good start. Whether it's a poor black family in Brooklyn or a poor white child in Kentucky, we must do more. Quite frankly, helping the poor is a moral imperative. Yes, it's good public policy but more than that, it's just the right thing to do.

42

STRENGTHEN THE FOOD STAMP PROGRAM

As a nation we need to work harder to address the underlying causes of poverty but in the meantime poor people need to have food on the table. The Food Stamp program is well worth the investment. People that can't afford to put food on the table deserve a helping hand. It's simply the right thing to do. Social conservatives often talk about America's Judeo-Christian heritage—as well they should. But what could possibly be more in keeping with that heritage than helping to feed the poor? Of course there are some people who abuse and defraud the system and we should crack down on such people and put them in jail. And of course we would much prefer to have a thriving economy where no one needs to rely on food stamps in the first place, but that's not always the case. Millions of people rely on this program and they should not be stigmatized for it. We must maintain a strong social safety net for those who truly need it.

43

CRACK DOWN HARD ON
WELFARE FRAUD

Yes, we must help the poor but we must stop letting people abuse the system. Too many people are looking to get a free lunch—literally. There are people with kids in public school who make plenty of money but have their kids signed up for free lunches. We need to crack down hard on all types of fraud, be it Medicare/Medicaid fraud, disability fraud, food stamp fraud, welfare fraud, etc. These programs are supposed to be there for poor people who truly need them, not for people who are just trying to milk the system for as much as they can get. More money and more resources need to be put into finding, arresting, and prosecuting those who commit welfare fraud. Anyone who gets food stamps or any type of welfare by hiding their income or assets should be swiftly and severely punished. They ought to be prosecuted to the fullest extent of the law.

44

CREATE MORE AFFORDABLE HOUSING

My childhood was spiritually rich but financially poor. Growing up let's just say things weren't always easy. These difficult experiences left an indelible imprint upon my mind and it because of them that I feel so strongly about doing more to help the poor, especially when it comes to affordable housing. The fact of that matter is that the lower middle class and the poor simply can't afford to pay the rent in many cities. A poor person who is working hard 40 hours a week at a low wage job is likely to see her entire paycheck go straight to the landlord.

What can be done? Here are a few ideas: First of all, get rid of all the public housing projects. Tear them down! These city housing projects crowd poor people together in ghettos where crime, despair, and dependency run rampant. Instead of the government spending billions of dollars administering and managing these gigantic public housing projects, simply allow people to rent from the private sector and provide the needy with a monthly stipend they can use towards their rent.

Another idea would be a legal requirement that *all* large scale landlords—those who own about 50 or more rental units— set aside at least 5% of their rental units for the poor. The rent for these units would of course be determined by the government and would be well below market value. In return, these landlords should receive property tax credits to help offset the money they will be losing on 5% of their units.

Last but not least, those who qualify for these affordable housing programs must be very strictly vetted. Too many people try to abuse the system. These programs must be kept for people who truly need them, not for people who are just trying to abuse the system.

45

CREATE A NATIONWIDE MENTORING PROGRAM

In America today there are far too many young people growing up in poverty and/or broken homes. If these young people just had proper role models in their lives they would reach their full potential. Too many kids grow up without a responsible parent to check their report cards, help them with their homework, and go to parent/teacher night at school. Too many young boys grow up without a father in their lives. Too many children come home to an empty house because they have only one parent and she has to work long hours. Let's be clear: nothing can replace the role of parents. First and foremost, kids need loving parents to act as proper role models; nothing can or should replace that. Sadly, however, many kids just don't have a stable family with loving parents. Every kid deserves to have a mentor—someone who they know cares about them, someone who believes in them, someone who will be a good role model for them.

We ought to have a national big brother/big sister mentoring program. Maybe we can call it "Mentors for America." All kids from disadvantaged backgrounds would be eligible. A disadvantaged background would mean kids from any single parent family and/or where the family is living below the poverty line. This idea doesn't have to become a massive new federal program; instead, the federal government could provide financial support to private charities that are already doing this type of thing. Yes, this idea might cost a little money in the short term but in the long term it will save the American taxpayer lots of money because we will have less kids winding up in jail and more kids finishing school. Kids with good role models tend to stay in school and stay out of jail and when they grow up they tend to become responsible citizens who will in turn be good role models for their own children.

46

STOP THE DOPING OF AMERICA'S CHILDREN

Did you know that little children as young as three years of age are now being prescribed powerful psychiatric drugs such as Ritalin and Adderall? Prescriptions for these types of drugs have skyrocketed over the last decade. As a society we are now engaged in the routine doping of children. Back in the old days when kids were a little rambunctious we had a name for that—childhood! That was part of being a kid. But now it's often considered a "disorder" for which the remedy is to just pop a pill. Even worse, in some cases parents are actually forced—through intimidation and coercion by the state—to give their kids these drugs against their will. These parents are sometimes told that if they don't go along with it they will be charged with medical neglect and their kids might be taken away from them.

While on the subject of the doping of America's children, a few things need to be said about the psychiatric establishment in general. The psychiatric industry has become too powerful and that power needs to be curtailed. Psychiatrists are the only doctors that can forcibly medicate people against their will. As a young law student, this writer worked with lawyers who represented people being held against their will in mental institutions. They were supposedly mentally-ill and a danger to themselves. What truly shocked me—and still shocks me—is that a citizen who is labeled as mentally-ill and alleged to be a danger to himself or others, actually has fewer rights than the worst of criminals. How so? First off, in order for an alleged criminal to be arrested in the first place he has to actually do something to break the law. The law calls this the "*actus reus*" element of the crime—the physical act itself. The cops can't just arrest someone because he fits the profile of a violent criminal and they think he might do something in the future.

When it comes to citizens alleged to be mentally-ill, it's just the opposite. In many states they can be locked up against their will, not based on anything they have already done, but on the mere predictions of what psychiatrists say they might do. In other words, in most states there is no requirement that they first commit a dangerous act. Yes, it's true that some people are criminally insane and they do need to be locked up. If a guy stabs somebody because he heard voices telling him to do it, such a person is criminally insane and they certainly need to be locked up. On the other hand, however, we should not lock people up based upon the mere predictions of psychiatrists—predictions that often turn out to be wrong.

We need to rein in the power of the psychiatric establishment and we need to let kids be kids. We need to stop the unnecessary doping of millions of young children and we also need to reform our mental health laws so that the due process rights of citizens are protected from a powerful psychiatric industry.

47

SHOW MORE KINDNESS FOR ANIMALS (ESPECIALLY IN THE MEAT PROCESSING INDUSTRY)

This idea, in all honesty, is not necessary to save America; however, it's necessary to make America a better, more ethical country—a country that lives up to her values. In Psalm 145 it says, "God is good to all, His mercies are on all His creations." Note the word, "all." We should emulate God and show compassion on *all* living creatures—even those about to be slaughtered for food. One need not be a vegetarian to be distressed by the cruel and harsh conditions animals have to endure at large meat-processing plants—one need only have sense of compassion. If these meat-processing plants were held to the same laws against animal cruelty as are applied to cats and dogs, everyone involved could be arrested on charges of animal cruelty. In the old days of small towns and small town butchers, animals were treated more humanely. Now we have gigantic factory farms that cram tens of thousands of animals together in crowded, cruel, filthy, and appalling conditions. If we are to remain true to our values then we should put a stop to this wanton cruelty against innocent creatures.

48

GET OFF FOSSIL FUELS

This is not going to happen overnight. It's going to take a long time to slowly wean ourselves off of fossil fuels but we ought to get serious about starting the process. There are several reasons why we need to do this. First of all, fossil fuels are a finite resource. There is only so much oil and coal in the ground and eventually, even it if takes 50 or 100 years, it will run out and it's not something we can ever reproduce. Our entire economy and society should not be dependent upon something that is certain to eventually run out and that we can't reproduce.

But there are even better reasons to get off fossil fuels. Much of our oil comes from countries in the Middle East that don't exactly share our values. Why is it that we call Saudi Arabia a "friend" and an "ally?" Clearly, the answer is that we depend upon Saudi Arabia for much of the oil that is the lifeblood of our economy and yet to say that Saudi Arabia doesn't share our values would qualify as the understatement of the century! They are an absolute monarchy and a strict Islamic theocracy. They subjugate women, treating them basically as a piece of property to be used by men. They execute people for their sexual orientation. They cut off people's hands for theft and they would not recognize freedom of speech or freedom of religion if it hit them in the face. The country is ruled by a bunch of inbred pedophiles and religious zealots. Last but not least, most of the terrorists who murdered 3,000 Americans on 9/11 were Saudi nationals. And yet, primarily because of our addiction to fossil fuels, we still call the Saudis our "friends." If not sending any more of our wealth to Saudi Arabia isn't a good enough reason to get off fossil fuels then nothing is.

Many intelligent people have argued that in order to stop buying oil from countries that hate us, we need to drill more here at home. There may be some truth to that. We need to wean ourselves away from fossil fuels but that is going to take some time. In the short term we probably should take an "all of the above" approach which means more drilling at home. If we're going to be addicted to oil, let us at least get that oil from American soil and support American companies and create American jobs. While more drilling at home might help in the short run, it's still just a temporary solution. The ultimate objective must be to break our addiction to fossil fuels once and for all and to develop clean, sustainable, and renewable energy sources.

Last but not least, we must break our addiction to fossil fuels because of the danger to the environment. The fact of the matter is that the great majority of scientists now believe that the use of fossil fuels is having a devastating effect on the Earth's climate. To be fair, this is not an entirely settled question. There are some distinguished scientists who believe that fossil fuels are *not* injurious to the environment and are *not* contributing to climate change. They believe that climate change is being caused by a myriad of other factors. Who knows? They might very well be right. Let's hope they are but in a case like this the prudent thing to do is to err on the side of caution. For all of these reasons, it's high time we break our addiction to fossil fuels once and for all! Let us now consider some ways to do just that...

49

INVEST IN CLEAN ENERGY—
SOLAR, WIND, WATER

The federal government spends (and often wastes) trillions of dollars each and every year. Why not take just a
tiny percentage of that money and invest in something
worthwhile? We need to break our addiction to fossil fuels
which are a finite resource and are most probably harmful
to the health our planet. We also need to stop supporting
Saudi Arabia and other hostile countries. A national investment in renewable energy would start us on the road
to accomplishing all of these goals. Yes, it will take quite
some time and yes, in the meantime we should probably
also allow for more drilling here at home but eventually we
need to find a permanent and safe solution. Energy that
comes from the sun, wind, and water is that solution. For
example, you have probably heard of the Hoover Dam.
The Hoover Dam provides about 4 billion kilowatt-hours
of clean hydroelectric power each year. This clean energy

is then pumped into millions of homes and businesses in Nevada, California, and Arizona. This is precisely the kind of thing we need to see more of—a lot more. It's time for America to get serious about clean renewable energy.

America is a gigantic country blessed with many types of climates. In the Southwest we have millions upon millions of acres of hot, dry, and very sunny deserts. In the Midwest we have the majestic Great Plains which also happen to be quite windy. Instead of depending on foreign oil, why not use our own resources to our advantage? We could build massive solar farms in the Southwest and windmill farms in the Midwest. These solar and wind farms could provide America with clean, renewable energy and help to begin the slow process of breaking our national addiction to fossil fuels. Who would build these wind farms and solar farms? Well, the federal government is not all that efficient. Perhaps there could be a joint public/private effort. Perhaps the federal government could provide tax breaks and some subsidies to get things started and then once the ball is rolling and it becomes profitable the private sector could take over. Or maybe instead of just handing out welfare checks we could reactivate the WPA and put people to work building up America's clean energy infrastructure.

We should also give people better incentives to drive fuel-efficient vehicles. On the one hand, the government should not tell people what they can or can't drive. If someone wants to drive a gigantic gas-guzzling SUV just because they feel like it, that is their choice and their right. But what the government can do is to give people strong incentives to drive cleaner vehicles. For example, in many places a person can now use the HOV lane if they are driving a fuel-efficient vehicle. This is a great idea. It gives people the freedom to drive what they want but it also provides an incentive to drive cleaner cars. The government should greatly expand on these types of incentives. People who drive cleaner vehicles should get free renewal of their vehicle registration and perhaps even a free yearly inspection. Perhaps owners of clean hybrid vehicles should also get a modest reduction on tolls when crossing bridges and tunnels, etc. We should also encourage more "green parking spaces." Just like handicapped parking is reserved with blue spaces, we should have parking spaces marked in green that allow owners of fuel-efficient vehicles to park right where they need to be.

Here's another idea: Let's install solar panels on every building in America. President Barack Obama spent almost a trillion dollars on his economic stimulus plan and what do we have to show for it? Where are all the public infrastructure improvements that were supposed to come from all of his "shovel ready jobs?" Putting solar panels on every building in America is certainly a very ambitious idea and it will surely cost a lot of money. But the federal government already spends a lot of money. Shouldn't we at least have something to show for it? We should make a concerted effort, using both the public and private sectors, to put solar panels on the rooftops of every single building in the country. This would certainly be a grand undertaking. Perhaps it's even unrealistic. But it's worth a try! Even if we can't get solar panels on every building, if we can even get a modest percentage of buildings outfitted with solar panels we could reduce our need for fossil fuels and create a permanent source of clean and renewable energy. If we could build the Hoover Dam at the height of the Great Depression, why can't we do this?

We were able to figure out a way to build atomic bombs that can incinerate the entire world 100 times over again and we were also able to put men on the moon. It seems that once Americans put their mind to something they tend to get the job done. If we could put the best and the brightest scientists together to figure out a way to build atomic bombs and if we could figure out a way to put a man on the moon, why can't we do the same thing when it comes to clean energy? We should have a new Manhattan Project but this time instead of bombs we will have the best and the brightest scientists coming up with new ways to get us off fossil fuels and to produce clean renewable energy.

50

PROMOTE SCIENCE AND TECHNOLOGY

"Space, the final frontier. These are the voyages of the starship Enterprise. Its five year mission: to explore strange new worlds, to seek out new life and new civilizations, to boldly go where no man has gone before."

The above passage will be quite familiar to any science-fiction fan, particularly "Trekkies." The great thing about Star Trek was that it encouraged us to dream big—*really* big. It was filled with optimism that science, along with the indefatigable human spirit, could take us to the farthest reaches of the universe. The promotion of science should be a national priority. A national commitment to promote science and technology will benefit all of us, not just Americans, but all of humanity. From space travel, to clean energy, to medicine, to things we can't even yet fathom, science will help take us there. The federal budget, at last count, comes to almost four trillion dollars per year. And yet, only a tiny fraction of that goes towards the study of science. This should change. We should have a new and bold national commitment to the promotion of science at all levels.

51

LEGALIZE DRUGS

The "war on drugs" has been a colossal failure. We waste billions and billions of dollars every year fighting this ridiculous war on drugs—a war we have already lost. As if that weren't bad enough, we have millions of people locked up in prison, often on non-violent drug charges. From the time of America's founding up until the early 20th century, drug use was not even regulated—much less criminalized—by the federal government. All of that has changed dramatically. The federal government, along with state and local governments, now spends tens of billions of dollars every year fighting this "war on drugs." Enough is enough. Let's just legalize drugs, period. They did it in Portugal and we can do it here too. We could still regulate drugs just as we do tobacco and alcohol. No one in their right mind would suggest allowing crack addicts to run amuck in our playgrounds or heroin addicts to shoot up outside of our schools and churches. The use of these dangerous drugs could and *should* still be regulated to keep them out of the hands of children and out of our residential communities. But at the end of the day, if someone wants to use drugs, so long as he or she is an adult of sound mind and so long as they are not committing any other crimes related to their drug habit, why the heck should the government have a right to stop them? In a free country, is it really any of the government's darn business?

If someone wants to throw their life away on drugs, it's really not the place of government to stop them. Freedom means being free to make stupid choices as long as you're not hurting anyone else. If you want to hurt yourself, that's your own business! If some people choose to abuse dangerous drugs that is their own stupidity. While we may have an ethical duty to try and help such people, it's really not the business of government to stand in the way. We can and should of course continue to punish those who operate motor vehicles while under the influence of drugs or who otherwise harm people or commit criminal acts. But the act of abusing drugs should itself not be criminalized. They legalized all drugs in Portugal over 15 years ago and there hasn't been an uptick in crime or drug abuse since. In fact, because of an emphasis on treatment instead of jail, drug abuse in that country has gone down. It's high time for America to realize that this "war on drugs" has been nothing but a disaster and a failure. We can do better.

52

RELEASE ANYONE INCARCERATED FOR A NON-VIOLENT DRUG CRIME

The amount of people locked up in prison in this country is staggering. There are well over two million Americans behind bars—more than any other nation in the world! America has about 5% of the world's population but almost 25% of the world's prisoners. Even China comes in only a distant second. Many of the people locked up have not even committed any act of violence but are locked up on drug charges. We waste billions and billions of dollars each year to keep all these people locked up. It is not a smart thing to do on a practical level and neither is it right on a moral level. Obviously, anyone who has committed an act of violence in the commission of a drug offense should stay in jail. We should have *zero tolerance* for violent thugs. We should also punish anyone who sells drugs to minors. But aside from that, all other non-violent drug felons should be released. Put them in treatment.

Put them on probation. Let them do some kind of community service. But let's stop throwing people in jail for non-violent drug offenses.

53

INSTITUTE A 5 YEAR MAXIMUM JAIL SENTENCE ON NON-VIOLENT CRIMES

The United States Constitution only lists three federal crimes: piracy, counterfeiting, and treason. The Crimes Act of 1790 added another 17 federal crimes. Today we don't even know exactly how many federal crimes there are. It is estimated that the federal criminal code contains more than 4,500 criminal offenses and the corresponding regulations put that number even higher—in the tens of thousands. This widespread criminalization of, well, just about everything, is certainly not what the Founding Fathers had in mind when they wrote the Constitution.

Firstly, we ought to drastically cut down on the number of federal crimes. Beyond that, we need to create more of a distinction between violent and non-violent crimes. People who commit non-violent crimes should be treated very differently from those who commit violent crimes. Yes, they should be punished but they should not be thrown in jail for decades. What are essentially property crimes such as mail fraud, grand larceny, money laundering, bank fraud, etc., should certainly be punished but not with ridiculously long jail sentences. First of all, those found guilty should of course have to pay back the value of whatever they stole—i.e. restitution. They should also have to pay a heavy fine, perhaps double or even triple the value of what they stole. On top of that they can be given long hours of community service to perform and can be put on probation for a number of years. However, in no event should anyone receive a sentence of imprisonment for more than five years on a non-violent property crime. Five years should be the absolute maximum and even that should only be reserved for the most wanton offenders.

54

SUPPORT THE POLICE

Most police officers should rightly be regarded as heroes. They deserve our high esteem, admiration, respect, and cooperation. Every day they leave the house and they literally put their lives at risk to keep our streets safe from dangerous criminals. If it were not for the great work of America's policemen and policewomen we would be in a lot of trouble. The vast majority of them are good and honorable and they don't deserve to be constantly demonized by the likes of Al Sharpton and his race-baiting friends.

However, with all that being said, sometimes the police do abuse their power and when they do they must be held fully accountable. Let's take something very minor and innocuous: cops who often violate the traffic laws by parking in front of fire hydrants or bus stops, using their cell phones while driving, etc. This might seem very minor but cops should always set the proper example. They should be role models of proper behavior. Just because a cop can get away with violating a traffic law does not make it right. They need to set an example and to obey the laws they are charged with upholding. A cop should be treated like any other American citizen. This means they should not be allowed to willfully violate the law, any law, even relatively minor traffic laws.

When it comes to more serious crimes involving police, there really needs to be more accountability. More accountability starts with every major city having a special prosecutor's office to deal solely with serious police misconduct. Why is this necessary? If anyone has ever watched an episode of the hit television show, "Law & Order SVU," they know that cops and the local district attorney work very closely together day in and day out. They're basically on the same team. How can a district attorney's office be fully impartial when prosecuting police officers with whom they have such a friendly and close relationship?

The simple answer is they probably can't. That is why every major city in America should have a special prosecutor's office that is fully independent from the local district attorney and deals only with allegations of serious police misconduct. Again, this is not to suggest that most police are corrupt or abusing their power. On the contrary, most police officers are honorable men and women who deserve our esteem and respect but if and when they violate the law they ought to be held fully accountable. This is America and no one is above the law, not the police, not the president, not anyone.

55

CRACK DOWN HARD ON VIOLENT CRIMINALS

When it comes to violent crimes we should have a zero tolerance policy. Society has a right to protect itself from dangerous criminals. We should not keep giving them a revolving prison door that allows them back out on to the streets only to rape, rob, and kill again. Those vicious criminals that commit rape, armed robbery, felony assault, murder, etc., should be dealt with swiftly and severely. Right now violent felons are often given a revolving door of parole, probation, and plea-bargains and are then back out on the streets only to rape, kill, and maim more innocent people. This must stop. No more revolving prison doors for violent felons. There should be a stiff mandatory minimum sentence on all violent felonies—no exceptions. At the same time, however, we should perhaps also focus more on rehabilitation. America now has one of the highest re-cidivism rates in the world. A whopping 75% of crimi-nals will commit crimes again and wind up back in jail. Punishment and deterrence are very important but we also need to do a much better job at rehabilitation.

56

PROVIDE HEALTH INSURANCE COVERAGE TO THOSE WHO CAN'T AFFORD IT

As previously stated, ending the war on drugs would save both the federal and state governments tens of billions of dollars. Drugs should also be taxed much in the same way that we tax cigarettes. We should then take some of the money saved from ending the war on drugs, combine it with all the new tax revenue, and then use that money to help people who lack health insurance. The working class and the poor deserve to have access to quality health-care, even if they can't afford it. As a society we have an ethical obligation to help them. America has always been a moral nation and providing good quality healthcare to all people, especially the poor, is a moral imperative.

57

GET RID OF THE INDIVIDUAL MANDATE PORTION OF THE AFFORDABLE CARE ACT

Many conservatives believe that the Affordable Care Act ("ObamaCare") must be completely repealed. This writer disagrees. The Affordable Care Act does not need to be repealed in its entirety. There are some parts of it, like cracking down on the insurance companies for instance, that make sense. Most Americans are kind and decent people who don't believe these companies should be allowed to deny coverage to a sick child just because he or she has a pre-existing condition. On the other hand, the individual mandate portion of the law must be repealed for it is a direct assault on personal liberty. It may have been upheld on a 5-4 vote of the Supreme Court (after Chief Justice Roberts somehow convinced himself that the fine imposed was really a tax) but it is flagrantly unconstitutional. It is also unprecedented. Never before in all the annals of American history has the federal government ever claimed the right to force a private citizen, minding his or her own business, to buy a product or service. This is a shocking attack on personal liberty. Where will it end? As Justice Antonin Scalia asked during oral arguments, if the federal government has the right to force citizens to buy health insurance, what *wouldn't* they be able to force us to buy? Would they be able to force us to buy broccoli? Bottom line: The individual mandate section of the Affordable Care Act is one of the worst attacks on individual liberty in our history and it must be repealed forthwith.

58

EMBRACE AMERICA'S JUDEO-CHRISTIAN HERITAGE

In 1774 the First Continental Congress assembled at Philadelphia. Do you happen to know the very first thing they did? They prayed. The Rev. Jacob Duche began the prayer with these words:

> *"O Lord our Heavenly Father, high and mighty King of kings, and Lord of lords, who dost from thy throne behold all the dwellers on earth and reignest with power supreme and uncontrolled over all the Kingdoms, Empires and Governments; look down in mercy, we beseech Thee, on these our American States, who have fled to Thee from the rod of the oppressor and thrown themselves on Thy gracious protection, desiring to be henceforth dependent only on Thee. All this we ask in the name and through*

the merits of Jesus Christ, Thy Son and our Savior."

Liberals are quick to remind us that America is a secular nation and that there is a separation of church and state. In some ways they're correct. From a purely legal standpoint this is not a Christian nation. The Constitution does not allow for the legal establishment of any religion and it prohibits any religious test for public office. So yes, from a legal standpoint America has no official religion but that doesn't tell the whole story. Culturally, sociologically, and historically speaking, America most certainly is a Judeo-Christian nation. The Judeo-Christian tradition has been inextricably intertwined with America since her very founding. As to the separation of church and state: yes, there is a separation of church and state and that is as it should be. However, that separation has never been absolute. I hat bears repealing. There has never been an absolute separation of church and state at any time in American history. A few quick examples:

- "In God We Trust" is our national motto and is emblazoned on courthouses and government buildings throughout the land. It has also appeared on some of our money as far back as the Civil War.
- Every session of Congress, going all the way back to the First Continental Congress in 1774 and

right up until today has opened with prayer. These prayers are led by an official chaplain who is paid by the treasury.

- The Supreme Court of the United States begins each session by invoking the name of God—"God Save the United States and this Honorable Court."
- Almost every president since George Washington has taken his oath of office on a Bible

The liberals are not happy about any of this. They want nothing less than an absolute 100% separation of church and state. They also want to destroy any remaining vestiges of the Judeo-Christian tradition in America. They seek to rewrite history to erase any and all evidence of the centrality of our Judeo-Christian heritage. If we are to save America we must put a stop to this assault on our heritage—a heritage that has been a bedrock foundation of who we are as a people. Instead of running away from our Judeo-Christian faith, we should embrace it. We should be proud of it! It is part and parcel of who we are as a country. Our Judeo-Christian heritage has sustained us and united us as a people since the birth of our nation. If our faith heritage offends certain people, too bad! If we are to save America we must save our Judeo-Christian heritage.

59

LET PARENTS (NOT GOVERNMENT) TEACH KIDS ABOUT "THE BIRDS AND THE BEES"

In major cities like New York, parents are now forced to have their kids attend mandatory sexual education programs. This is wrong. Parents should be able to raise their children as they see fit. The government has no business forcing parents to put their kids in sex education classes. Ideally, it should be left up to parents to teach their kids about the "birds and the bees" and to instill in them the morals that they see fit. However, at the very least, parents should have an absolute right to pull their kids out of these classes. Also, before giving their consent parents should be informed as to precisely what their children will be taught. It's high time for the government to stop infringing on the rights and prerogatives of parents.

60

RESTORE AMERICA'S TRADITIONAL VALUES

Traditional values? Some will laugh at this one. Some people scoff at the notion of traditional values. The truth of the matter is we've become rather depraved as a society. Traditional values need to be reinvigorated into all facets of American life. Just look at television as an example. Way back in the 1950s we had television shows like *Leave It To Beaver* where the kids all sat down at the dinner table together every night and often addressed their father as "Sir." On *I Love Lucy*, the show's main characters, Lucy and Ricky Ricardo, were often shown in two separate beds even though they were married. Even into the late 1960s and early 1970s we had wholesome shows like *The Brady Bunch*, where kids still had respect for their parents and for themselves.

Today society has undergone a radical transformation. It is now considered the norm for kids to disrespect their parents and teachers. Sexual promiscuity is now the norm. Divorce is now the norm. Absentee fathers are now the norm. Abortion is now the norm. Profanity is now the norm. Lewdness is now the norm. A radical redefinition of family is now the norm. Having sex-change operations at the taxpayer's expense is now the norm. In short, anything goes! If it feels good, do it. Traditional values have been replaced by total moral relativism.

If we are to start to save America we have to begin to put the brakes on all this. We have to try to somehow slowly bring back traditional family values. We have to instill a sense of decency, modesty, and morality into kids. We have to say no! No, disrespecting your parents and teachers should *not* be the norm. Sexual promiscuity should *not* be the norm. Profanity in our speech should *not* be the norm. Absentee fathers should *not* be the norm. Abortion should *not* be the norm, etc. This process won't be easy since we're already so far gone as a society. But maybe if we work together one person at a time, one family at a time, one church at a time, one synagogue at a time, perhaps we can somehow begin to change the tide and begin the journey back to the traditional values our nation once cherished.

61

BAN PARTIAL BIRTH ABORTION

This is a heinous procedure. It is not simply an abortion. It is infanticide. It involves a doctor actually delivering a portion of a living child outside of the mother's body and then killing it. In a head first delivery, the baby's entire head would be outside of the birth canal. The baby is then killed when the doctor crushes its skull or suctions out its brain. This is pure barbarism and should be banned. The only exception should be if the physical health of the mother is in imminent danger.

62

RESTORE A RESPECT FOR LIFE (*ALL* LIFE—INCLUDING BABIES IN THE WOMB)

On the one hand, the government should not have the power to tell a woman what she can or can't do with her own body. The unborn baby (no, I will *not* call it a "fetus") is still in her body and a part of her body. In a free country we must tread very carefully when it comes to telling a person what to do with their own body. On the other hand, abortion is absolutely detestable. The idea of deliberately killing an unborn baby in the womb is morally repugnant. It should shock the conscience of all decent and civilized people everywhere. Unfortunately, it does not shock our conscience anymore because America has lost her way. We no longer respect the sanctity of life. The fact that there have been not less than 55 million abortions since Roe v. Wade should leave us all shocked and horrified. Over 55 million babies killed in the womb! But it doesn't even bother us anymore. People just don't seem to give a damn. Some people look at killing babies in the womb as a simple choice, like the choice to dispose of an old chair one no longer has any use for. Others see it as a method of population control. My goodness! America has reached unfathomable depths of perversion when we can look at the killing of babies with such a cavalier attitude.

Many in the pro-life movement want to repeal Roe v. Wade but what will that accomplish? First of all, we should be very wary of a government telling someone what they can or can't do with their own body—even if that action is morally repugnant to us. But putting that aside, even if Roe v. Wade vanished tomorrow, many states would still choose to allow abortion on demand and in the ones that don't, women will find a way to have the abortions anyway—likely at secret abortion clinics that are unlicensed and dangerous. If we are to truly protect the unborn child in the womb we must begin to somehow restore a respect for life. As a society we must once again find our humanity. We must learn to cherish and respect all life—including the lives of unborn children in the womb. We must also not blame the woman—after all it takes two people to make a baby. We must help women who are not ready to care for children to realize that there are other options, such as adoption, that are readily available to them. But above all we must once again restore a respect for the miracle and sanctity of life!

63

PROTECT RELIGIOUS LIBERTY

There can be no doubt that religious liberty is under assault. All over the country religious Americans are being told to either give up their right to own a business or give up their religious values. Liberals in the gay rights movement are now going after private businesses that refuse to support same-sex marriage. An Oregon bakery, owned by religious Christians, was fined $135,000 dollars for refusing to bake a wedding cake for a lesbian couple. That bears repeating: $135,000 dollars for simply not baking a cake! People of faith are now being told to choose between their religious convictions and their livelihood. Isn't this precisely what the 1st Amendment is supposed to protect us against? Doesn't it say that government may not prohibit the "free exercise of religion?" What has this country come to when a religious Christian or a religious Jew is allowed to be persecuted simply for staying true to his or her religious beliefs? If the courts will not uphold the 1st Amendment then individual states need to pass religious freedom laws to protect people of faith from this new type of persecution.

64

SAVE THANKSGIVING

Thanksgiving was my grandmother's favorite holiday. She loved freedom and she loved America and she was always thankful. I guess that's why I'm partial to this holiday. What's not to love about Thanksgiving? It's a uniquely American holiday, a holiday of food, family, and football. It's a day to be thankful to God for our country, for our families, for our freedom, and for all our blessings. Sadly, too many employees are now being forced to spend Thanksgiving away from their families. In the not too distant past, it would have been unheard of for a store to be open on Thanksgiving. Sure, "Black Friday" sales started very early on the Friday morning after Thanksgiving, but at least the stores we're not open on the holiday itself. More and more stores are now opening on Thanksgiving Day itself, forcing millions of employees to be away from their families. Thanksgiving should be a day for all American families to stay home and be together, not to have wild stampedes at the mall so we can get a new flat-screen TV at 50% off! It is simply un-American for stores to be open on Thanksgiving. Let us all resolve to save this uniquely American holiday!

65

STOP THE WAR ON CHRISTMAS

This one doesn't require much explanation. Many people today are somewhat afraid of Christmas. They're afraid that if they celebrate Christmas too publically they will somehow be doing something wrong. Maybe someone will be offended. They're told they need to be more "inclusive." Some public schools will not even allow children to sing Christmas carols anymore. Nativity scenes are being taken down left and right. What used to be called Christmas break is now called winter break and Christmas parties are now called holiday parties. Some stores won't even let their employees wish customers a "Merry Christmas." Enough is enough. It's time to stop this war on Christmas!

66

FORGET PRESIDENT'S DAY— BRING BACK WASHINGTON AND LINCOLN'S BIRTHDAY

America used to celebrate the birthdays of arguably her two greatest presidents, George Washington and Abraham Lincoln. Then someone came up with the bright idea of "President's Day" which is probably the dumbest and most meaningless national holiday ever invented. Instead of taking the time to pause and honor the two presidents but for whom America would probably not exist, we celebrate the meaningless and amorphous "President's Day." Let's get rid of this silly holiday and bring back Washington and Lincoln's birthday celebrations.

67

GET RID OF POLITICAL CORRECTNESS

Political correctness is a disease of the mind—a mental disorder if you will. It primarily affects liberals but the ramifications of it are felt far and wide. Political correctness is a totalitarian ideology that tells you how to think, what questions you may ask, what things you may believe, what books you may read, and what speech you may use. It also puts feelings ahead of facts. If the facts conflict with how we feel about a certain issue then those facts must be either ignored or distorted. Make no mistake, political correctness is destroying our freedom and if we're to save America it must be totally wiped out!

Political correctness works by trying to silence any and all dissenting voices. It seeks to shut down debate before debate even starts. For example, if you're not quite convinced that Islam is a perfectly peaceful religion then you are "islamophobic" and you must be silenced. If you don't fully support gay marriage then you are a "homophobe" and you must be silenced. If you are critical of anything in the black community (and you happen to be white) you are a "racist" and you must be silenced. If you want to crack down on illegal immigration you must be a "xenophobe" and you must be silenced. The basic idea is censorship. If you don't support the liberal agenda then they will try to punish you and silence you at all costs. Although liberals may claim otherwise, make no mistake, they most certainly do not believe in the principle of free speech. They believe in silencing any and all opposition. They will even come after your job or your business in an effort to shut you up.

Want proof? Just ask Pat Buchanan who was fired by the ever so tolerant liberals at MSNBC because he dared to write a book they didn't approve of. Or you can ask Juan Williams who admitted that people in Muslim garb on airplanes sometimes make him a bit nervous. The liberals at NPR fired him almost instantaneously and suggested that he see a psychiatrist. You could also speak to Lawrence Summers who was forced out as President of Harvard University for having the audacity to ask some questions that the feminists didn't like. Or perhaps speak to Brandon Eich who was forced to resign as CEO of Mozilla because he dared to donate a few bucks to a ballot initiative in California that reaffirmed the traditional definition of marriage. These are but a few examples of political correctness run amuck. It is quite evident that political correctness and freedom are completely antithetical to each other. Indeed, the liberals who support political correctness are nothing more than well-meaning fascists.

The absurd rules of political correctness also state that a white person is never, *ever*, allowed to be critical of non-white minorities. Break this rule at your own risk for they will label you a "racist" and come after you like a wild mob with pitch forks. On the other hand, the rules of political correctness dictate that racism against whites, especially white Christian males, is perfectly okay.

The famous documentary filmmaker and ultra-liberal Michael Moore wrote a book entitled *Stupid White Men* in which he goes through all the supposedly pernicious activities of the moronic and evil white male. Since Moore's racism and sexism was targeting white men, the rules of political correctness were on his side. The book discusses all the terrible things Moore says the "white man" has done and the liberals just love that kind of thing but imagine if he were to list some terrible things done by blacks. Imagine if he instead had called the book *Stupid Black Men.* That would have been the end of his career. In the liberal's worldview it's fine to paint white men in a negative light while simultaneously highlighting the achievements of minorities. Under the bizarre rules of political correctness racism can only emanate from white people against non-white minorities and only non- white minorities are permitted to take pride in their cultural achievements.

To sum up, these are but a few examples of the disease of the mind known as political correctness—a disease that is destroying our country. There is but no question that freedom of speech is under attack in America today. The people who support political correctness will stop at *nothing* to silence any and all dissent. The lunatic liberals and their cult of political correctness are destroying freedom of speech in a way that no army ever could. The Founding Fathers wanted us to live in society that was open to the free exchange of ideas—whether or not we agree with those ideas. Whether it is Michael Moore, Al Sharpton, the feminists, or the gay rights folks, they're basically all the same—they demand censorship and will try to silence any dissent. They only want free speech if it is speech they deem acceptable and appropriate.

It is time for us, the American people, to stand up to these lunatics. We will no longer be silenced! We will not be scared of their labels or their threats or their intimidation. We will speak our minds and tell it like it is. We must no longer be afraid of these politically correct mobs. We will stand up to these people because we must. Freedom of thought depends on it. Freedom of speech depends on it. Our country depends on it. If we are to save freedom and to save America we must eradicate this plague of political correctness once and for all!

68

CONFRONT AND DESTROY
RADICAL ISLAM

Liberals stubbornly refuse to admit that we are engaged in a war against the dark and savage forces of radical Islam. They practice willful blindness and willful ignorance when it comes to the true source of terrorism and violent extremism. They can't bring themselves to directly confront radical Islam because to do so offends their left-wing sensibilities and their notions of political correctness. In their bizarre world we have just as much to fear from religious Christians and even the Tea Party, as we do from radical Islam. President Barack Obama made a speech on the threat from ISIS (the Islamic State in Iraq and Syria) in which he stated that "ISIS is not Islamic." Secretary of State John Kerry has declared, "ISIS has nothing to do with Islam." Not to be outdone, Hillary Clinton has declared that Muslims "have nothing whatsoever to do with terrorism." Not Islamic? Nothing to do with Islam? Really? Then just who in the hell are these bloodthirsty terrorists? Buddhists? Quakers? Southern Baptists? Let's get real!

Obama and the liberals constantly lecture us that Islam is a "religion of peace." Many Americans are quite fed up with liberals telling them how Islam is a "religion of peace" while they see radical Muslims chopping people's heads off, burning people alive, blowing up buildings, raping women, hijacking airplanes, and committing all manner of atrocities on every continent of the globe while shouting "Allah Akbar!" To be clear, this is *not* to suggest that all or most Muslims are violent. That is clearly not the case. It is very important to remember that there are many good and decent Muslims out there. It would be unfair to stereotype all Muslims based on the actions of some and we must be careful not to do that. However, we must also face up to reality and realize that there is a problem of violence within Islam today.

Be it a café in Australia, a synagogue in Denmark, a parliament house in Canada, a newspaper office in Paris, a train in London, an airport in Brussels, a dance club in Orlando, or a World Trade Center in New York, we find these Jihadist savages on the attack all over the world. In addition to all of that, radical Islam is a religion that still puts gay people to death, oppresses women, punishes premarital sex with 180 lashes, condones pedophilia, and teaches youngsters that killing innocent people in suicide bombings will send them straight to heaven.

While it's certainly true that most Muslims are not terrorists, it is equally true that most terrorists profess to be Muslims. It is also a fact that according to numerous polls, a substantial percentage of Muslims tacitly support, condone, and excuse violence committed in the name of their religion. Again, to be clear, there are many peaceful and good Muslims out there who hate the radicals as much as anyone. We should never forget that. However, we can't ignore the reality that there is a substantial percentage who do indeed support the radical Jihadist mindset. They might not be terrorists themselves but they support the terrorist's Jihadist ideology. They might not shoot or stab someone for insulting Mohammad but they sympathize with the one who does. Consider these numbers:

- 35% of French Muslims and 24% of British Muslims admit to believing that suicide-bombings against civilians are justified if intended to "defend Islam."
- After the heinous attacks upon the London subway and bus system in 2005, the BBC conducted a poll which found that near nearly 25% of British Muslims believed the attack was justified because of Britain's involvement in Iraq and Afghanistan.
- According to a spring 2015 Pew poll, 20% of Muslims in Nigeria hold a favorable view of the Islamic State—ISIS
- According to that same Pew poll, only 28% of Muslims in Pakistan expressed an unfavorable

view of ISIS. 62% had no opinion and 9% expressed favorable views

We must cut out the silliness when it comes to the politically correct nonsense that radical Islam is not at war with the West and that it's not the root cause of terrorism. How can we defeat an enemy when we are not even allowed to name that enemy? If it were 1940 would Barack Obama declare that Germany is a nation of peace? Would John Kerry tell us that Nazism has nothing to do with Germany or the German people? Professor Samuel P. Huntington was right when he famously predicted that there was going to be a "clash of civilizations." Radical Islam is clashing with modernity. It is threatened by it and seeks to destroy it—to destroy *us*. So let's cut the crap. No more political correctness. Enough is enough! If we are to save America (and the rest of the Western world too) then we must boldly confront radical Islam, declare war upon it, and utterly destroy it!

69

USE PROFILING WHEN NECESSARY TO PROTECT THE NATION AND SAVE LIVES

In 2011 the New York Police Department came under criticism for "spying" on Muslims. The NYPD had apparently been keeping certain mosques under surveillance and in some cases had even sent undercover officers to infiltrate these mosques. Liberals of course cried foul. The basic question is this: Should America's law enforcement agencies have an aggressive anti-terrorism strategy that includes an increased focus on certain parts of the Muslim community? In other words, should they profile? The answer is yes.

Before liberals start screaming about "Islamophobia" let's be crystal clear that most Muslims in this country do not support terrorism. Indeed, the majority of Muslims are good and decent Americans. On the other hand, we must not hide from reality – even if that reality is politically incorrect. The fact is that although most Muslims are not terrorists, a large and disproportionately high number of Muslims have been involved in terrorist attacks and terrorist plots. To put it plainly, while most Muslims are not terrorists, most terrorists are Muslim. Be it a Jew, Christian, Muslim, Hindu, it makes no difference. If violence is coming from a certain community then logic dictates that the police should focus more attention and resources on that community.

The U.S. State Department maintains a list of major terrorist attacks around the world. The fact of the matter is that radical Muslims are disproportionately represented on that list. Muslims account for the majority of terrorist attacks throughout the world. According to a 2013 report by the Heritage Foundation, there have been at least 60 terrorist plots right here in the United States since 9/11. Those plots weren't hatched by radical Catholics, radical Buddhists, or radical Mormons. Why is it so hard to face the truth? The answer is that some liberals are driven by a fanatical ideology of diversity and multiculturalism. They don't wish to be bothered by facts. Facts tend to get in the way of their tidy view of things but as John Adams once said, "Facts are stubborn things."

Liberals bemoan the supposed evils of profiling and demand that police put a stop to it. Put a stop to what? To thwarting terrorist plots? To keeping us safe? They suggest that law enforcement is engaging in some sort of sinister activity that unjustly punishes all Muslims. That is just not the case. The police are in fact protecting all

Americans – Muslim and non-Muslim alike – from homicidal maniacs. The NYPD was simply following the evidence and adjusting their strategy accordingly. To do otherwise would be irrational and foolish.

We know at least one thing about profiling – it works. It works because contrary to what liberals us, it's not based on racial or ethnic animus. It is based on math, statistics, and most of all, a healthy dose of common sense. El-Al is Israel's national airline. El-Al doesn't just profile, they profile with gusto! They don't just racially profile. They ethnically profile, religiously profile, sexually profile, linguistically profile, and just about any other type of profiling you can think of. They aren't ashamed of it. And do you know why? Because it works! There has not been a successful terrorist attack on an El Al plane since 1968.

In short, it's time for liberals to stop hiding from reality. While we must never forget that most Muslims are law-abiding citizens, we can't ignore the facts. The threat posed by Islamic extremism is as real as it gets—bombs don't discriminate. Instead of criticizing law enforcement for using profiling to keep us safe, we should be thanking them!

70

STAND UP FOR HUMAN RIGHTS AROUND THE WORLD

Let's be honest. America has made some mistakes in our past and we've sometimes acted like hypocrites. This is especially true with regard to our foreign policy post-World War II. As one who loves America deeply, it hurts to admit that we have sometimes put our economic interests ahead of what is right and just. In some cases our CIA has helped to overthrow democratically elected governments. We have kept silent in the wake of human rights violations by certain countries. We have sometimes turned a blind eye to the atrocities of dictators. For decades we have been rolling out the red carpet for the communists in China who would not know a human right if it hit them in the face. Because of our addiction to oil, we've made friends with Arab states (like Saudi Arabia) that treat women like dirt, persecute and often murder gay people, and believe that anyone who criticizes Islam should be put to death. Some of these countries have been a breeding ground for terrorists—Osama Bin Laden was a Saudi and so were 15 of the 19 hijackers on 9/11.

This is not said lightly nor is it said to bash America. It is said because this writer loves America and wants America to live up to her values at all times and without exception. If we are to fulfill our destiny and be that "shining city upon a hill" then we must stand up for liberty all around the world—without exception. Yes, it is true that America has stood up for freedom against the Nazis and against the Marxist onslaught during the Cold War. We have helped to liberate hundreds of millions of people. Indeed, we have a lot to be very proud of. But that's not good enough. America shouldn't stand up for human rights and liberty some of the time or even most of the time, America should stand up for human rights and liberty *all* of the time!

The basic protections of individual liberty as outlined in our Constitution and Bill of Rights are not just American rights, but are the God-given natural rights of *all* human beings. Any nation that does not respect basic human rights such as freedom of speech, freedom of religion, freedom of the press, etc., should never be called an ally of the United States. On the contrary, any nation that does not respect the basic liberty and human rights of her people should be treated as an enemy of freedom and, therefore, an enemy of the United States.

71

WORK EVEN HARDER TO REDUCE CIVILIAN CASUALTIES

America and the West are in a war against the forces of radical Islam and sometimes in a war innocent people get killed; however, we need to do even more to reduce civilian casualties. Every time we hear about innocent children getting killed in a drone strike our hearts should break. To be clear, America already does try to limit civilian casualties. Unlike the radical Muslims, the American people are a moral people; we don't try to kill innocent people and we don't take any pleasure when it happens. But maybe we need to do even more. We should work even harder to make sure innocent civilians are not getting killed—albeit accidently.

In the past, two armies would meet on the field and give battle. Soldiers got killed. Civilians, for the most part, did not. In the Battle of Gettysburg, which was the greatest military battle in the Western Hemisphere, there were over 50,000 military casualties and yet only one civilian was killed. With the advent of air power all of that has changed and sadly civilian deaths occur all the time now. It is true that we are in a clash of civilizations, fighting against the forces of darkness, but the ends cannot justify the means. We are fighting the forces of darkness and so we must continue to be the light unto the nations. Let us resolve to confront and destroy radical Islam but let us also resolve to remain a moral people and a people that do absolutely everything in their power to prevent harm to civilians.

72

CLOSE DOWN THE PRISON
AT GUANTANAMO BAY

No one detests radical Islam and the terrorists who believe in it more than this writer. But right is right and wrong
is wrong. As Americans we don't believe in indefinite de-
tention without trial. That goes against everything this
country stands for. If we sacrifice our values to fight terrorists then what are we fighting for? The Magna Carta was
signed in the year 1215. For the first time, people thrown
in jail had a right to a trial by a jury of their peers. Later on
England also gave us the "Great Writ," the Writ of Habeas
Corpus which declares that no one can be held in jail without being brought before a court to challenge their de-
tention. These important principles were later codified in
our Constitution and Bill of Rights.

So what do we do about the detainees at Guantanamo?
We should have done one of two things from the start:
either treat them as prisoners of war or put them on

trial before a civilian or military court. If we treat them as POWs they should be afforded the full protection of the Geneva Conventions. Once the war is over they should be returned to their respective countries. For example, once major combat operations have ended in Afghanistan and our troops have been pulled out, that part of the war is over and all detainees from Afghanistan should be sent back.

The second option would be to simply charge these people with any crimes they have may have committed and give them a full and fair trial either before a civilian court in the United States or before a military tribunal. If they are tried before a military tribunal it should be a court-martial that would afford them the same protections any American solider would receive under the Uniform Code of Military Justice. It must not be a kangaroo court either. We are better than that. Kangaroo courts are fit for third-world dictatorships, not for the greatest country on Earth. Some of the prisoners at Guantanamo might be detestable miscreants but even detestable miscreants have rights. Their due process rights must be protected at all times. They deserve a right to counsel, a right to be confronted with the witnesses against them, a right to cross-examine those witnesses, and a right to bring forth witnesses and evidence in their defense. By protecting their rights we are standing up for our American values and setting a proper example for the world. Not only that, we'll be making certain that we are in fact punishing the right people and that justice is truly being served.

The bottom line is that holding people in prison indefinitely and without trial is simply un-American. It goes against everything this nation stands for. It is beneath us and it needs to stop.

73

FIND AND SECURE ALL "LOOSE NUKES"

One of the dangers we face today is a nuclear catastrophe. As of now, nine countries have nuclear weapons and a number of others have stockpiles of highly enriched uranium. We certainly don't have much to worry about when it comes to countries like Great Britain or France; however, what about countries like North Korea? What about Pakistan? What about the thousands of nuclear warheads, plutonium, and highly enriched uranium floating around the former Soviet Union? What if any of these "loose nukes" fell into the wrong hands? Would Islamic extremists hesitate to use them? A nuclear detonation in a major city would be a catastrophe beyond our ability to imagine. Even a small "dirty bomb" which spreads radioactive material over a city would be an unprecedented calamity.

The United States, along with our allies, must do everything in our power to see to it that this never, ever, happens. This should be one of our top national security and foreign policy priorities. We must work together with other nations to secure all nuclear weapons and fissile material. Be it money or manpower, we must spare no expense and do whatever it takes to fully secure all of these materials. Even a 99.9% success rate is not good enough. Just one nuclear weapon falling into the wrong hands would be an unthinkable disaster. The United States government along with the rest of the civilized world must do whatever it takes to make sure that never happens.

74

WORK TOWARDS A NUCLEAR-FREE WORLD

Perhaps this is too hopeful and unrealistic at the present time. We live in a very dangerous and chaotic world and for the present moment America must maintain a strong nuclear deterrent. But is this what we want to leave our children and grandchildren, a world that can still be instantly destroyed by the push of a button? Can't we at least dream of a better world? Can't men and women of good will get together and figure out a way to rid this planet of nuclear weapons? And if we can't fully get rid of them, can't we at least greatly reduce the amount of them? How many thousands of nuclear warheads does this world really need? Maybe this is just a dream, but wouldn't a nuclear-free world be a great gift to leave to our posterity?

75

STRENGTHEN NATO

The North Atlantic Treaty Organization, formed after
World War II, has been one of the great alliances in the
world. For decades, NATO stood as a bulwark against
Soviet totalitarianism in Europe. While it is true that
George Washington warned us against "entangling alliances," NATO has been a great success. It has been a
success because it has united many of the civilized nations of this world—nations that respect individual liberty,
democracy, and the rule of law. We live in a dangerous
and often chaotic world. China is building up their military
and becoming more belligerent. North Korea has atomic
weapons and is run by a bunch of lunatics. The Middle-
East is an utter mess. Radical Islam is a worldwide threat.
The freedom-loving nations of this world must continue
to stick together. No, we can't be the world's policeman
and we can't get involved in every conflict but at the same
time we can't hide our heads in the sand either. We live

in a world of intercontinental ballistic missiles, chemical weapons, and cyber-terrorism. We must resist the calls of isolationists and we must strengthen our commitment to NATO.

One other thing to keep in mind: of all our NATO partners and allies we should always remember our special relationship with Great Britain. The United States shares more in common with the British than with any other country in the world. Not only do we have a common language but we also have a common history, a shared set of values, a shared legal tradition, and many other things that make for an unshakeable bond between the United States and the United Kingdom.

76

ENCOURAGE OUR FRIENDS IN EUROPE TO STOP COMMITTING NATIONAL SUICIDE

It is in America's best interest to have strong, stable, and secure allies. Our closest allies in Western Europe are all facing a serious problem. They are committing national suicide. The problem is particularly bad in France where that nation now has a population that is almost 10% Muslim. Because of the liberal obsession with multiculturalism, Europe is on the road to ruin. The people of France are not having very many children. At the same time new waves of Muslim immigrants are having lots of children. While it remains true that most Muslims are good and decent people, it doesn't take a genius to figure out what will eventually happen to Europe. As the old saying goes, "demography is destiny."

These are sovereign nations and so we can't tell them what to do but as a friend and ally we need to speak out and strongly urge the nations of Western Europe to stop committing national suicide. They need to substantially reduce immigration from Muslim countries. They then need to insist that all new immigrants fully assimilate. They also need to immediately deport any immigrant who expresses support for terrorism. Last but not least, the nations of Western Europe have very low birth rates and they need to start having more children. The choice is simple: They can either do these things or they will eventually commit national suicide. Most of Europe will become a Muslim continent. What the invading Muslim armies could not do in the 7th and 8th centuries, demographics will do in the 21st. Let's urge our friends and allies to not let that happen!

77

STAND UP TO CHINA

Aside from the Dalai Lama, it seems like the only one willing to really stand up to China is Donald Trump. Trump has his faults—lots of faults—but on this issue he's absolutely right. Trump does not mince words when it comes to China. He has said that China is "raping this country" and is "our enemy." Is Trump correct? Let's look at the facts. China is a rising power and, at best, a strategic competitor to the United States. The Chinese government has a track record on human rights that is abysmal to say the least. The basic human rights that any decent American cherishes—freedom of the press, freedom of speech, freedom of religion, due process of law, etc.—are virtually non-existent in China. In addition, China has engaged in and continues to engage in massive cyber-warfare against the U.S. and has stolen many of our technologies. They have manipulated their currency to gain an unfair trade advantage against other countries. They have ruthlessly oppressed and persecuted the people of Tibet. They continue to threaten Taiwan, have become increasingly belligerent towards Japan, and are now making ridiculous territorial claims in what are international waters of the South China Sea. But perhaps most alarmingly they are also militarizing at a quick rate. China now spends more money on their military than any other country besides the United States. Let's be clear: China is nothing more than a belligerent bully that is seeking to surpass America in terms of economic, political, and military power. We must *not* allow that to happen!

78

MAINTAIN AMERICA'S
MILITARY SUPREMACY

It is a self-evident truth that peace is preferable to war. Certainly we all wish that there could be peace on Earth and we should all fervently hope and pray for that great day. But in the meantime we must maintain a strong military—*the* strongest—because when push comes to shove the world looks to America for leadership. While we can't be the world's policeman, we can and must see to it that our military remains the strongest and most technologically advanced in the world—bar none. We must be ready to meet any and all threats to our national security and to protect freedom. China is right now greatly expanding and strengthening her military. We must never allow China or any other nation to overtake us when it comes to military power. Will China protect freedom? When the chips are down, freedom-loving people all over the world will still look to America for help. We must see to it that the land, naval, and air forces of the United States of America continue to be the strongest in the world.

79

BE PREPARED FOR A WMD
OR CYBER-ATTACK

We live in a very dangerous and chaotic world. What makes the world particularly dangerous nowadays is that there are weapons out there that could wipe out millions of people in the blink of an eye. Never before in human history have there been chemical, biological, and nuclear weapons that could kill so many people so quickly. The motto of the Boy Scouts is, "Be Prepared." That's a good motto. The United States must do everything in her power to be prepared for an attack by terrorists using weapons of mass destruction. We must first and foremost do everything in our power to prevent such an attack from ever happening in the first place. But we should also be fully prepared to respond to such an attack should it ever, God forbid, take place. A terrorist attack using chemical, biological, or nuclear weapons would make 9/11 look like a picnic! This is quite probably the single greatest threat to our national security. Does anyone doubt that if terrorists got a hold of these weapons of mass destruction they would not hesitate to use them? Does anyone doubt that terrorists are actively trying to get their hands on these types of weapons? There is no simple quick-fix for this one. We just can't let our guard down. We can't become complacent. We must be ever vigilant. As the Boy Scouts say, we must "be prepared."

Also, in addition to the threat of a WMD attack we now must be prepared for a cyber-attack. We now live in an electronic and digital age and so the threat of a cyber-attack is very real and we need to be a lot more prepared for that as well. Just imagine if terrorists or a rogue state took down our whole banking system or our internet in a cyber-attack. We can't allow that to happen.

80

REQUIRE UNIVERSAL BACKGROUND CHECKS AND GUN SAFETY TRAINING

We must always uphold the 2nd Amendment. Any law-abiding citizen who wishes to possess a gun has a right to do so. However, no right is absolute. Thousands of innocent people are murdered with guns every year and tens of thousands are injured. There are some simple things we can do right now that would save lives while still fully upholding the 2nd Amendment.

The idea of universal background checks and gun safety training should really be a "no-brainer." It's just pure common sense. For example, we require people to take a certain amount of training, including a written test, an eye test, and a road test in order to obtain a driver's license. We also require that the automobile be registered and inspected for safety. Why should it be any different when it comes to firearms? The overwhelming majority of Americans support universal background checks. And one more thing, an individual's mental-health must be part of the background check. We don't want people with serious mental problems having access to guns. Of course, a person deemed unfit because of an alleged mental-illness must have his due process rights protected and should be able to challenge this determination in a court of law.

Yes, we absolutely have a constitutional right under the 2nd Amendment to own guns and yes law-abiding citizens should most certainly be able to protect themselves and their families. The 2nd Amendment is as important and sacred as any other part of our Constitution but what is so bad about having to undergo a background check and some gun safety courses? Yes, law-abiding citizens should be able to own guns but criminals should not. Background checks and safety training are perfectly reasonable requirements that ought to precede any firearms purchase. When a person decides to become a police officer they don't just hand him a gun on the first day. First they must pass a background check. Then they are given proper training in the safe handling and use of firearms. There is no reason not to require something similar for any citizen who wishes to own a gun.

81

PASS "SHALL ISSUE" LAWS IN EVERY STATE

As previously stated, anyone wishing to purchase a gun should first have to undergo a full background check and take a training course on gun safety. Just as a person must pass a written test and a road test to drive a car, a potential gun owner should have to demonstrate that he or she knows how to safely and properly handle firearms. However, once a person has undergone the proper background checks and safety training, he or she should immediately be issued a permit to keep guns in the home and/or to carry them on the streets. Gun ownership is not just privilege; it is our *right* under the 2nd Amendment of the Constitution of the United States. This right is currently being violated in many states and cities all over America. We should therefore enact "shall issue" laws in every state. Once a citizen has undergone the requisite training and background checks, the state shall issue him a gun permit forthwith. It should not be left to the discretion of any administrative agency or government bureaucrat.

Moreover, in addition to protecting the 2nd Amendment, allowing and encouraging law-abiding citizens to own guns is good public policy. Think of it this way: in America today we have around a million people who carry guns every single day and nobody has a problem with it. They are called police officers! Why is it that we trust police officers with firearms but not just a regular law-abiding citizen? This makes no sense. Police officers aren't angels. They're human beings like everyone else. Why should we trust them with guns any more than we would an ordinary citizen? The only real difference is that the police officer has probably undergone an extensive background check and has been given proper training in the use of firearms. This is as it should be. But if a citizen is willing to undergo a similar background check and similar training, why should he or she not be allowed to carry a concealed weapon? We have a hell of a lot more to fear from violent criminals (who always seem to get the guns anyway) than we do from law- abiding citizens. Yes, we certainly need to do a heck of a lot more to keep guns out of the hands of criminals. But try as we might the bad guys still seem to get guns and as the saying goes, the only thing that will stop a bad guy with a gun is a good guy with a gun.

82

CRACK DOWN HARD ON THOSE WHO SELL GUNS ILLEGALLY

Anyone caught dealing in the illegal sale of firearms should be punished swiftly and severely. Many guns fall into the hands of dangerous predators and vicious thugs because they are purchased legally and then resold illegally on the black market. These "straw purchases" result in guns falling into the hands of gang members, rapists, and killers. The authorities, both federal and state, need to step up enforcement and crack down hard on this. In addition, a new law should be passed that imposes an automatic and mandatory jail sentence of not less than 5 years for *anyone* involved in the illegal sale of a gun—no exceptions.

83

PUNISH LAWYERS WHO ABUSE THE LEGAL SYSTEM WITH FRIVOLOUS LAWSUITS

Let's be honest, there are a lot of sleazy lawyers in this country. That's not to say all lawyers are sleazy. There are certainly plenty of outstanding and honorable members of the legal profession. However, our legal system as a whole has been compromised. Something simply has to be done about all of these frivolous lawsuits. One could write a whole book just on all the utterly frivolous and ridiculous lawsuits in America. These frivolous lawsuits have made a mockery of our legal system and they have to be stopped. Not only that, the cost to the American taxpayer is enormous. In New York City alone, over 500 million dollars a year is spent just to settle lawsuits. One of the best ways to put the brakes on such frivolous lawsuits is to punish the lawyers who file them. Most states and the federal courts already have sanctions that can be imposed on lawyers who file frivolous lawsuits but these sanctions are seldom imposed. It's time that they start imposing these sanctions and they ought to make them more severe. Maybe if these sleazy lawyers actually had to worry about losing their license to practice they might think twice about suing McDonald's because their clients are too fat!

84

SET UP A "LOSER PAYS" SYSTEM

This is a very simple rule and it would really help to curb all the frivolous lawsuits that are undermining our once great legal system. The rule should be that in any lawsuit over $50,000 dollars, the losing side should have to pay the reasonable expenses, including attorney's fees, of the winning side. The losing plaintiff should be on the hook for 50% and the losing plaintiff's attorney should be responsible for the other half.

85

PROVIDE INDIGENT DEFENDANTS A RIGHT TO COUNSEL IN SOME CIVIL CASES

A poor person should be given a free lawyer in certain cases. Why? It's simply the right thing to do, that's why. Most people know that a person who is arrested and can't afford a lawyer must be provided with one. This is as it should be. However, what about civil cases? There are some civil cases that can have very serious repercussions and it's only right and fair that a poor person be provided legal counsel in such cases. If an indigent defendant is being brought to court by the government (for whatever reason) he or she should be given a lawyer. For example, if the state is trying to force a mother to medicate her child for an alleged psychiatric problem, she deserves a lawyer. If the state is trying to confiscate someone's property through civil forfeiture or eminent domain, they deserve a lawyer. If the state is trying to have someone committed to a mental institution, they deserve a lawyer. Basically, anytime the power of the state is brought to bear against an indigent citizen, he or she deserves to be provided legal counsel. Even in some private litigation, it is only right and just that indigent defendants be given a lawyer. For instance, if a landlord is trying to throw a tenant out on the street and the landlord is represented by a lawyer then it's only fair that the tenant should have a lawyer too—in other words level the field and make it a fair fight.

One important condition for this rule: the indigent person should have to provide clear proof that he or she is, in fact, indigent. They should have to provide bank statements, tax returns, pay stubs, etc. Too many people know how to milk the system and will pretend to be poor just to get a free lawyer. Anyone caught hiding assets or income should not only not get a free lawyer but should be prosecuted and thrown in jail.

86

HAVE STRICT TERM LIMITS ON ALL ELECTED OFFICIALS

Without a doubt, we absolutely need to put strict term limits on all elected officials. We have far too many career politicians who get far too comfortable in their cushy jobs and are far too removed from the people they are supposed to serve. Some of these politicians have never even held down a real job in their lives. They become more interested in accumulating power and prestige than in serving their constituents and (barring some sort of scandal) it's almost impossible for a new guy to defeat an incumbent in a primary. We desperately need to pass a constitutional amendment that would impose strict term limits on both the House of Representatives and the Senate—perhaps not more than 12 years in either body. Furthermore, state legislatures are important too. We need state constitutional amendments imposing similar term limits on *all* state legislators, governors, and even local politicians. Throw the bums out!

87

CREATE A "PEOPLE'S VETO" FOR SUPREME COURT DECISIONS

This nation, as Abraham Lincoln once said, is supposed to be "a government of the people, by the people, and for the people". Regarding the Supreme Court, Lincoln said the following on March 4, 1861: "…the candid citizen must confess that if the policy of the government, upon vital questions affecting the whole people, is to be irrevocably fixed by decisions of the Supreme Court…the people will have ceased to be their own rulers, having to that extent practically resigned the government into the hands of that eminent tribunal."

While the Supreme Court serves a very important role and while an independent judiciary is absolutely essential, it's time to return some of the power back to the people. As a matter of fact, the first three words of the Constitution begin with, "We the People." The Supreme Court sometimes makes very good decisions but it has also made some horrendous decisions. All too often we now have federal judges who legislate from the bench; that is, rather than merely *interpreting* the Constitution in accordance with the original intent of the Framers, they seek to impose their own personal values and opinions upon it. This is simply not the job of a judge and we need to put a stop to it.

We must also ask ourselves why decisions of the Supreme Court are now considered sacred and beyond debate. Thomas Jefferson was absolutely furious with the decision in Marbury v. Madison. In that famous case, the Supreme Court took upon itself the power of judicial review—a power not actually mentioned in the Constitution. Jefferson didn't think any one branch of the government should have more power than the others when it comes to upholding the Constitution. It really comes down to this: in a country that prides itself on democratic values, is it sensible to allow 9 people in black robes to make decisions that will bind over 320 million?

Let there be proposed a new amendment to the Constitution that would create a "People's Veto" of Supreme Court decisions. To be clear, this is not something we should take lightly. The Supreme Court is a very important institution and we must continue to have an independent judiciary. In general, we should respect Supreme Court decisions, even if we may disagree with them. But what if a decision is particularly egregious? What if the whole country is outraged by it? Should a small handful of people have the final say over the lives of hundreds of millions? The proposed amendment would work like this: if a 2/3 majority of both houses of Congress or a 2/3 majority of the legislatures of the several states agree that a decision of the Supreme Court violates the original intent of the Constitution, said decision would be still be binding on the parties to the case but it would be nullified as far as setting any legal precedent upon the rest of the nation.

88

AMEND THE CONSTITUTION TO PROVIDE A "STATE'S VETO" OVER FEDERAL LEGISLATION

The idea of federalism and state's rights has been severely diminished. The notion of a federal government that only has the right to act based upon powers that are expressly enumerated in the Constitution is almost a joke nowadays. Ask most people about the 10th Amendment and you are likely to get a blank stare. The Founding Fathers most certainly did not intend to have an all-powerful federal government that would have plenary power over virtually all aspects of our lives.

The 10th Amendment declares the following: "The powers not delegated to the United States by the Constitution, nor prohibited by it to the States, are reserved to the States respectively, or to the people." Ever since the 1930's and continuing right up until today, the interstate commerce clause under Article I Section 8 has been used to poke holes in the 10th Amendment—so many holes that it practically looks like a hunk of Swiss cheese. In a nutshell, anything that is said to have the slightest effect on interstate commerce, no matter how remote or indirect, is then said to fall under the federal government's power to regulate interstate commerce.

It's time to bring back the important principle of federalism and to do this will require a new amendment to the Constitution. The proposed amendment would be as follows: if the States believe any federal law goes beyond the rightful jurisdiction of the federal government (in violation of the 10th Amendment), the individual state legislatures may then vote to nullify the law. If 3/4 of the States agree, the federal legislation would be null and void.

89

APPOINT JUDGES WHO WILL
RESPECT THE CONSTITUTION

This one is quite simple. We need judges who have a healthy respect for the Constitution. We need strict constructionists on the federal bench— judges who believe in following the original intent of the Framers of our Constitution and who will not seek to impose their own values upon it. We need judges who know that their proper role is interpreting the law rather than creating it— judges who can be trusted to uphold the original meaning of the Constitution and not legislate from the bench.

90

ENACT STRICT VOTER I.D. LAWS IN EVERY STATE

What do a 6-pack of beer and a library card have in common? Simple: to get either one you might need to provide some kind of identification. It doesn't stop with just beer and library cards either. Air travel, hotel reservations, opening a bank account, renting an apartment, applying for employment, and many other things nowadays all require photographic identification. Why should it be any different when it comes to voting?

Voting is one of the most important things a citizen can do. It is a citizen's sacred right and civic duty. It is of fundamental importance in any republic. But voting is a privilege reserved for citizens and only citizens. If just anyone can walk in off the street and register to vote it undermines the entire process. If an illegal immigrant can just fill out a form and register to vote it's not only unlawful and wrong but it undermines public trust in the whole system.

Each state needs to pass strict voter I.D. laws. Anyone registering to vote should have to produce some identification and proof of citizenship. When it comes time to go down and vote at a polling place they should have to produce photo identification there too. What about citizens that are elderly or live in rural communities where it might not be so easy to get proper I.D.? This is definitely an issue that needs to be addressed. To remedy this, six months before any election each state should have an affirmative duty to reach out to rural communities, poor communities, the elderly, the homeless, and others who may not have proper identification. They should have to go into these communities and work hard to make sure everyone can get proper I.D. (free of charge). What about a citizen who, for whatever reason, still does not have proper I.D. on Election Day? Should he or she be turned away? No. But he or she should have to swear out an affidavit certifying his identity and his status as a U.S. citizen. His photograph and fingerprints should also be taken. Thereafter, his identity should be fully investigated by state authorities and if he has lied that would be voter fraud as well as perjury and such a person should be prosecuted to the fullest extent of the law.

91

ENACT CAMPAIGN FINANCE REFORM

Money is power. That's just a fact. If people aren't rich enough to finance their own campaigns, they must go on bended knee to one of the major political parties to seek their endorsement. But what if a person is an independent, not beholden to either political party? Well, if he's worth 30 billion dollars like a Michael Bloomberg, he can simply finance his own campaign. What about the rest of us? The average American certainly doesn't have the money to self-fund a campaign.

There needs to be a way for average Americans to run for elective office even if they aren't millionaires and billionaires. The democratic process works best when *everyone* gets to participate. Our democracy should not revolve around just two political parties that one must submit to in order to run for office and neither should our democracy be in the hands of a few wealthy people who call all the shots. Not everyone can afford to attend $10,000 dollar a plate political fundraisers at the Waldorf.

It's time we had a system of public financing for political campaigns. Anyone who gets enough signatures to get on the ballot should automatically get a certain amount of public financing for his or her campaign. They could still raise private funds as well but at least this way everyone would have some money to get their campaign started and their name before the public. In addition, any candidate on the ballot should get a certain amount of time on the public airwaves, free of charge.

To be clear, private donations to candidates from private citizens should still be completely legal—it's a matter of free speech. The private contributions, however, should be totally transparent. The voters should be made aware of exactly who is donating what money to what candidate. Last but certainly not least, we should stop treating corporations like people. They aren't people and therefore don't deserve the same rights as people. They are legal entities designed to maximize shareholder profits and there should be a limit on how much money any one corporation can contribute to any one candidate. We want our elected officials to be answerable to the American people, not to some powerful international corporation.

92

ELIMINATE FELONY DISENFRANCHISEMENT

If a person is locked up for committing a crime then he or she should not have the right to vote during that time. Most people would agree that it's perfectly reasonable and fair to restrict the voting rights of convicts while they are incarcerated. But what about after they get out? In many states, people are disenfranchised long after they get out of jail. This is not right, nor is it good public policy. Once a person does his time and gets out of jail our goal should be to integrate them back into society—not to further alienate them. Felony disenfranchisement is unfair, undemocratic, and it's time to end it.

93

REQUIRE MANDATORY CIVICS EDUCATION FOR ALL STUDENTS IN ALL SCHOOLS

In order to drive a car one needs to demonstrate some knowledge about cars. In order to become a high school history teacher one needs to demonstrate some knowledge of history. In order to become a doctor or lawyer one needs to demonstrate knowledge of medicine or law. In many states you even need a license to cut someone's hair or give them a massage. Voting is the most important thing a citizen can do. Having informed citizens who take part in the electoral process is of fundamental importance in a representative democracy. And yet, despite the great importance that voting entails, at the age of 18 any natural born citizen can register to vote without having to demonstrate even the slightest knowledge of our laws, history, or government.

Timothy M. Rosen

A new constitutional amendment is necessary because education should normally be left up to the states but this issue is too important and there must be a national standard. The proposed amendment would require all students in all schools, both public and private, to be taught basic civics. This would include things like separation of powers, checks and balances, federalism, the Constitution and Bill of Rights, the Declaration of Independence, the Founding Fathers, the American Revolution, etc. Before graduating from high school every student should have to take and pass a basic civics exam, similar to the one we give to new immigrants before they can become U.S. citizens.

94

FORCE CONGRESS AND THE WHITE HOUSE TO FULLY DISCLOSE *ALL* FINANCIAL DEALINGS

We need to have a lot more truth and transparency in our government. The American people have lost faith in government and for good reason. They are fed up with corruption, kickbacks, nepotism, sweetheart deals, etc. We need a new law that would require *all* members of Congress (as well as their top aides) and *all* top officials within the executive branch to fully disclose (by sworn affidavit) all of their income sources, financial dealings, stocks, ties to corporations, and off-shore accounts—literally everything. This information should have to be updated every year and should be published on the internet for all to see. If they have nothing to hide then there should be no problem with disclosing such information to the American people. In addition, similar laws need to be passed for all politicians at the state level as well.

95

PASS A LAW BANNING COMPLICATED LAWS

President Obama's Affordable Care Act is almost 1,000 pages long. But wait! That's not all! The regulations under the Affordable Care Act come out to almost another 11,000 pages. Let me repeat that: 11,000 pages of regulations for just this one law! The official code of federal regulations, the CFR, now stands at a whopping 169,000 pages and counting. Again, that's worth repeating: 169,000 pages! This is astounding and it needs to stop.

Let's pass a very simple new law: all federal laws must be written in plain-English and shall be no more than 25 pages long. And as far as the corresponding regulations, they shall be no more than 100 pages. That's it. Let's keep it simple. If Congress can't seem to pass laws that aren't less than 1,000 pages long then maybe these laws should not be passed in the first place!

96

BRING BACK INDIVIDUALISM AND PERSONAL RESPONSIBILITY

America used to be a nation that promoted individualism and personal responsibility. Sadly, this is all too often not the case anymore. Nowadays people are told not to depend on themselves but to depend on the government. To be clear, we certainly should have a strong safety net for those who fall on hard times and we have a moral imperative to help the poor; however, this should not mean that we create a society of perpetual victims and perpetual dependency.

One of the things that made America great was our strong belief in personal responsibility and freedom—our frontier mentality. The famous historian Frederick Jackson Turner declared that it was the frontier—the wide-open lands of the West—that molded the American character into what it is. A poor man could go out West and stake his claim. By virtue of his own strength, ingenuity, and spirit, he could make a life for himself and his family. He had no one to rely on but himself and God. This kind of "rugged individualism" had a profound impact on America. The old cowboy of the West believed in freedom and personal responsibility—he was his own man. He did not rely on farm subsidies or government programs. The only person he relied on was himself. When things went well he could claim credit for it. When things did not go his way he blamed no one but himself. He loved God, country, and family. Most of all he loved freedom. He loved that he had the freedom to make his own destiny. He was the cowboy, the frontiersman, the pioneer. And, according to Turner's thesis, it was this type of pioneer spirit that became ingrained in the American psyche—it made us who we are.

Today we are losing our frontier spirit. Instead of being responsible for ourselves, the liberals declare that if things don't go your way it's not your fault. It's always somebody else's fault. Rather than take responsibility for yourself, just blame someone else. Blame the government. Blame the wealthy. Blame your parents. Blame white people. Blame the police. But whatever you do, never blame yourself. On the one hand, yes, we certainly do have a moral obligation to help the poor. Does more need to be done? Sure. Is the ever widening gap between rich and poor troubling? It certainly is. The problem with liberals, however, is that they see government as the only solution to all problems while simultaneously downplaying the vital importance of personal responsibility.

It is true that some poor people are the victims of circumstances beyond their control but others are victims of their own stupidity and poor choices. Liberals want to tell us that all financial problems are basically caused by greedy white men. If a person is poor it can't ever be their own fault. The liberals indoctrinate the poor not with the "can do" spirit of America but with a mentality of hopelessness, government dependence, and perpetual victimhood. How can someone take control of their own life and their own destiny if liberals constantly brainwash them to believe that without government assistance they are basically helpless? This writer happened to grow up poor but I was *never* taught to blame others. I was taught to have a positive outlook, work hard, and trust in God—never to blame others or to become bitter.

If our republic is to survive we must bring back the notion of personal responsibility. For over 200 years America held fast to the notion that we're all ultimately responsible for our own actions and our own lives. We have to restore a sense of personal dignity and responsibility in people instead of creating a society of perpetual victims. We need to return to the Turner Thesis. We need to return to that very American notion of "rugged individualism" that made America great. We need a society that is more like the Old West—a society that relied on individual grit, self-reliance, and tenacity. We need a little less Oprah Winfrey and a little more John Wayne.

97

SAVE THE CONSTITUTION

"We the People of the United States, in order to form a more perfect Union, establish Justice, insure domestic Tranquility, provide for the common defense, promote the general Welfare, and secure the Blessings of Liberty to ourselves and our Posterity, do ordain and establish this Constitution for the United States of America."

There are 101 ideas in this book on how to save America but few of them are more important than this one. This one is absolutely essential. We have a Constitution of the United States that is supposed to be the supreme law of the land. All elected officials swear to uphold it and yet our Constitution is being violated in so many ways by so many people one could write an entire book on the subject. As a matter of fact, someone has. For a more a detailed examination of how our Constitution is being eviscerated, read *Men In Black* by Mark Levin. It's a great book that every American who cares about the Constitution needs to read. Whether it's the right to bear arms under the 2nd Amendment or the principle of federalism and state's rights under the 10th Amendment, it's time to start respecting and obeying the Constitution once again. Whether it's a president signing "executive orders" that usurp the proper law-making power of congress, a National Security Agency violating the privacy rights of citizens, or judges who willfully ignore the original intent of the Framers, it has to stop. If we are to have any chance of saving America we've got to start by saving our Constitution.

We start with voting. We must elect only those politicians who have a proper respect for the United States Constitution. We must elect only those people who understand the importance of a *limited* government and who will appoint judges that respect the Framers of the Constitution and will seek to follow their original intent. We need judges who will uphold the inalienable rights guaranteed by the Constitution but at the same time we need judges who will not invent new "rights" out of thin air—rights that are not found anywhere in the Constitution. We must have leaders who will respect all the amendments in the Bill of Rights—including the 10th Amendment. When it comes to the Constitution, we need to elect a president that is the exact opposite of Barack Obama—a president that would not dare act like a tyrant. We need a president that would not dare to say, "If Congress won't act, I will." We need a president that would not dare violate federal immigration laws with an unconstitutional executive order or claim the right to hold American citizens indefinitely and without trial.

It is also time to seriously consider a new constitutional convention—a convention of the States under Article V. The mechanism for such a convention is quite simple: upon the application of 2/3 of the legislatures of the several states, a constitutional convention would take place. Things are already so far gone and the Constitution already so compromised that this may be our last resort and best hope of turning things around. Mark Levin, in his book, *The Liberty Amendments,* has clearly laid out the necessity and urgency of an Article V convention of the States and the movement is beginning to gain traction.

America is slowly slipping down the road towards tyranny. We need swift and bold action to save what is left of our country. Our Constitution—the heart and soul of who we are as a nation—is being distorted, ignored, violated, and slowly ripped to pieces. If we are to save America then we must save the Constitution!

98

SAVE OUR FREEDOM

*"Freedom is never more than one gen-
eration away from extinction."*

—Ronald Reagan

What does America represent if not freedom? Freedom is America and America is freedom. America is supposed to be the "land of the free." American patriots from the times of the Revolutionary War and right up until today have been willing to lay down their very lives in defense of freedom. A love of freedom is at the core of who we are as Americans. As Patrick Henry once said, "Give me liberty, or give me death!" But today freedom is under attack. That much is certain. Not only are many of our constitutional freedoms being violated, but lunatic liberals have created a climate of fear—fear that having the wrong thoughts, asking the wrong questions, or voicing the wrong opinions will get a person fired from his or her job or put out of business. This is a result of political correctness—a doctrine that should be repugnant to freedom-loving people everywhere. How can people be truly free if they are afraid to speak their minds? If a religious Jew or Christian voices her opposition to gay marriage she is immediately smeared by the Left as a homophobic bigot and her job and livelihood might be in jeopardy. If someone dares to mention the link between radical Islam and terrorism he too will be attacked and scared into silence. How can freedom survive in such an atmosphere? And then on top of all that we have those who wish to impose a "nanny-state" upon us. They want the government to have more and more power over the individual. They truly believe that most people are just too stupid to run their own lives and need government to do it for them.

Whether it's a federal government (for the first time in history) forcing private citizens to purchase a service whether they like it or not, state governments forcing parents to send their kids to mandatory courses on sex and "gender identity," an EPA telling us what kind of light bulbs we may use, or a mayor trying to tell us what size soda we may buy, freedom is under constant attack. If we are to somehow turn back the tide and save America we must save and protect our freedom. We must stand against those who wish to impose upon us the tyranny of political correctness. We must also band together and elect only those politicians who respect our natural, God-given right to individual liberty. We must begin to take down the nanny-state apparatus brick by brick. How will we do all this? It will be a long and hard process. The enemies of freedom are on the march and they won't stop unless we stop them. Can we do it? It won't be easy. But for the sake of all the patriots who came before us and for the sake of future generations, we have to try!

99

SUPPORT GROUPS THAT ARE ALREADY WORKING TO SAVE AMERICA

There are already many fine organizations that are working hard to save America but they can't do it alone. They need our help and we must all do our part. Here is a short list of just a few of the terrific organizations that are fighting to save America. Check out their websites and look into them for yourself. Be as generous as you possibly can. These worthy organizations are on the front lines in the battle to save America and it's our duty to do all we can to help them!

- The Young America's Foundation
- The Federation for American Immigration Reform
- The Landmark Legal Foundation
- The American Center for Law and Justice
- The Tea Party Patriots Citizens Fund
- The Institute for Justice

101 Ways to Save America (Before It's Too Late)

- The Foundation for Individual Rights in Education
- The David Horowitz Freedom Center
- The Heritage Foundation
- Judicial Watch

100

FIGHT!

*"Perseverance and spirit have done won-
ders in all ages."*

-GENERAL GEORGE WASHINGTON

America is at a tipping point. In fact, we might already be
past the tipping point. We need to save America and we
don't have much time left. Things are already so far gone.
Our Constitution, our traditions, our values, our faith, our
borders, our language, and our culture are all under attack. Meanwhile, a monumental national debt is crushing
us. This book lists many ways to save America. Perhaps
not every suggestion in the preceding pages is realistic
or wise. You be the judge. But let's be clear: if we don't
act soon America as we know it will be gone. That's right.
There will be no America left to save. The America we
know, the America that served as that beacon of hope,

as that "shining city on a hill," will be gone forever. Some may feel that it's already too late, that things are already too far gone and maybe we should just throw in the towel. But that's not the American way. As Americans, optimism, resoluteness, grit, and courage are in our DNA. We don't just give up. We don't throw in the towel. We fight. And when we aim to fight we aim to win! As John Paul Jones once said, "I have not yet *begun* to fight!" So, let's do it. Let's fight to save America—before it's too late!

What to do? We need to get organized at the grassroots level. There are still millions upon millions of patriots who love this country. We still have great power if we just *use* it. It's up to you and me and every single one of us to do our part. Will you just put this book aside and let it gather dust, or will you stand up and take action? It's not just about voting, although voting is extremely important. We also need to dedicate our time, our money, and our minds to saving what is left of our country.

We can start by joining local groups in our communities. We can take our country back inch by inch. This is a new civil war. It can be fought first and foremost at the ballot box, but also in the courts, in the media, and in the universities. We can talk to our neighbors. We can get together with our churches and synagogues. We can talk to our fellow citizens at work and at the local pub. We can write letters to newspapers. We can use social media like Twitter and Facebook. We still have freedom of speech, let's use it! It will take an all-out effort by every single patriotic American to save what is left of this country. So let's do it! Let's get organized and let's fight! During the American Revolution, the Founding Fathers pledged "our lives, our fortunes, and our sacred honor." Over 620,000 Americans were killed during the Civil War. Another 400,000 Americans sacrificed their lives for freedom during the Second World War. Don't we owe it to the memory of all the patriots that came before us to at least try to save America? Don't we owe it to the future generations who will come after us?

101

PRAY

This might just be *the* most important suggestion of all. America has already reached a tipping point. Things are already so far gone in so many ways. Perhaps more than anything else what America needs most is a great spiritual revival. How can we save America if not through the grace of God? As it says in Scripture, "Blessed is the nation whose God is the Lord." Let us pray that we can still save America. Let us pray that America can once again be that "shining city on a hill." Let us fervently pray and declare our faith that this great experiment in human liberty will not end and that "government of the people, by the people, and for the people, shall not perish from the earth."

EPILOGUE

This book has tried to make the case that our nation is in very serious trouble and that we must take immediate action to save America before it's too late. Our constitution, our liberty, and our core values are all being destroyed. As our heritage of freedom is being stolen, our borders, language, and culture eviscerated, will you just stand idly by? If you love America and you don't want to see your country destroyed then it's up to you to take bold action! It's up to each and every one of us to do his or her part. We must act now and do whatever it takes to save America before it's too late—and make no mistake, it will soon be too late. If you're a patriot who still loves America then when you put this book down you will stand up—stand up and take action! You may not agree with all the suggestions outlined in the preceding pages, but surely you agree with some of them. Pick the areas that you feel strongly about and get moving! We cannot afford to delay or to be half-hearted in this fight. The future of our country is at stake.

WORKS CONSULTED

INTRODUCTION

- Mark R. Levin, *Liberty and Tyranny* (New York: Simon & Schuster, 2009).

SECURE THE BORDER

- Senator Jim DeMint, "Finish the Border Fence Now, Human Events", May 17 2010, http://humanevents.com/2010/05/17/finish-the-border-fence-now/.
- Federation for American Immigration Reform, "Mexico's Defense of Illegal Immigrants," July 2005, http://www.fairus.org/site/PageServer?pagename=iic_immigrationissuecenters_defense.
- Vincente Fox and Rob Allyn, *Revolution of Hope* (New York: Penguin Group, 2007), 339.

- James C. McKinley Jr.," Mexican President Assails U.S. Measures on Migrants," New York Times, September 3, 2007, http://www.nytimes.com/2007/09/03/world/americas/03mexico.html?_r=0.
- Steven A. Camarota, "Immigrants in the United States, 2007: A Profile of America's Foreign Born Population," Center for Immigration Studies, November 2007, http://cis.org/immigrants_profile_2007.
- J. Michael Waller, "Mexico's Immigration Law: Let's Try It Here at Home," Human Events, May 2006, http://www.humanevents.com/article.php?id=14632.

FINGERPRINT AND PHOTOGRAPH EVERY SINGLE PERSON COMING INTO THIS COUNTRY

- Laura Ingraham, *Power to the People* (Washington: Regnery, 2007), 63.

CUT OFF ALL FUNDING TO SANCTUARY CITIES

- Jillian Jorgensen, "Council Passes Bills to Stop Cooperation with Federal Immigration Detainers," New York Observer, October 22, 2014, http://observer.com/2014/10/council-passes-bills-to-stop-cooperation-with-federal-immigration-detainers/.

- Lornet Turnbull, "More States Issuing Driver's Licenses to Those in U.S. Illegally," Seattle Times, June 22 2013, http://seattletimes.com/html/localnews/2021250610_driverslicensexml.html.
- Catherine E. Shoichet and Tom Watkins, "No Green Card? No Problem -- Undocumented Immigrant Can Practice Law, Court Says," http://www.cnn.com/2014/01/02/justice/california-immigrant-lawyer/index.html.

DECLARE ENGLISH AS OUR OFFICIAL LANGUAGE

- Alexander Hamilton, James Madison, and John Jay, *The Federalist Papers* (1787), Garry Wills, ed. (New York: Bantam Books, 1982), 7.
- Patrick J. Buchanan, *State of Emergency* (New York: St. Martin's Press, 2006), 72.

PROMOTE AMERICANISM INSTEAD OF MULTICULTURALISM

- Patrick J. Buchanan, *State of Emergency* (New York: St. Martin's Press, 2006), 13.
- Carol Iannone, "How Muslim Footbaths Threaten America's Social Fabric," New York Daily News, February 2008, http://www.nydailynews.com/opinions/2008/02/13/2008-02-13_how_muslim_footbaths_threaten_americas_s.html.

EMBRACE THE IDEA OF AMERICAN EXCEPTIONALISM ONCE AGAIN

- Larry Schweikart and Michael Allen, *A Patriots History of the United States* (New York: Penguin Group, 2004).

TEACH KIDS TO RESPECT AMERICA'S FOUNDING FATHERS

- Ron Chernow, *Washington: A Life* (New York: Penguin Press, 2010).
- David McCullough, *John Adams* (New York: Simon & Schuster, 2001).
- Mike Tobin, "Activists Set Sights on Schools Named for Slave-Owning Founding Fathers," FoxNews.com, May 11 2001, http://www.foxnews.com/story/2001/05/11/activists-set-sights-on-schools-named-for-slave-owning-founding-fathers/.

STOP THE LIBERAL INDOCTRINATION OF AMERICA'S SCHOOLCHILDREN

- Robby Soave, "Students, It's Illegal to Wear an American Flag Shirt on Cinco De Mayo," dailycaller.com, May 5 2014, http://dailycaller.com/2014/05/05/students-its-illegal-to-wear-an-american-flag-shirt-on-cinco-de-mayo/.

- Robert Schaffer, "Seattle Schools Thanksgiving 'Myths' Stir Controversy," FoxNews.com, November 22 2007, http://www.foxnews.com/story/2007/11/22/seattle-schools-thanksgiving-myths-stir-controversy/.
- CNN Wire Staff, "California Governor Signs Bill Requiring Schools to Teach Gay History," CNN.com, July 15 2011, http://www.cnn.com/2011/US/07/14/california.lgbt.education/index.html.
- Madeleine Morgenstern, "Texas Teen Suing School District After She Was Punished for Not Reciting Mexican National Anthem in Class," theblaze.com, February 28 2013, http://www.theblaze.com/stories/2013/02/28/texas-teen-suing-school-district-after-she-was-punished-for-not-reciting-mexican-national-anthem-in-class/.
- Fernanda Santos and Anna M. Phillips, "New York City Will Mandate Sex Education," the New York Times, August 9 2011, http://www.nytimes.com/2011/08/10/nyregion/in-new-york-city-a-new-mandate-on-sex-education.html?_r=0.

ELIMINATE SOCIAL PROMOTION AND INSIST ON HIGH STANDARDS IN EDUCATION

- The New York Times Editorial Board, "The United States Falling Behind," the New York Times, October 22 2013, http://www.nytimes.com/2013/10/23/opinion/the-united-states-falling-behind.html.

- Franchesca Warren, "Too Many Students Rely on Social Promotion," the Huffington Post, September 29 2014, http://www.huffingtonpost.com/franchesca-warren/social-promotion-is-not-a_b_5896120.html.

INSIST ON INTELLECTUAL DIVERSITY AMONGST UNIVERSITY FACULTY

- Larry Scholer, "Faculty Conservatives Outpolled Again," academia.org, April 5 2005, http://www.academia.org/faculty-conservatives-outpolled-again/.
- Scott Jaschik, "Moving Further to the Left," insidehighered.com, October 2012, https://www.insidehighered.com/news/2012/10/24/survey-finds-professors-already-liberal-have-moved-further-left

FIRE COLLEGE PROFESSORS WHO ATTEMPT TO INDOCTRINATE THEIR STUDENTS OR VIOLATE ACADEMIC FREEDOM

- David Horowitz, *Indoctrination U: The Left's War Against Academic Freedom* (New York: Encounter Books, 2009).
- American Association of University Professors, 1940 Statement of Principles on Academic Freedom and Tenure

- American Association of University Professors, Joint Statement on Rights and Freedoms of Students

GET RID OF AFFIRMATIVE ACTION

- Clarence Thomas, *My Grandfather's Son—A Memoir* (New York: HarperCollins, 2007), 74-75.

PASS A BALANCED BUDGET AMENDMENT TO THE CONSTITUTION

- Mark Knoller, "National Debt Has Increased More Under Obama Than Under Bush," CBS News, March 19 2012, http://www.cbsnews.com/news/national-debt-has-increased-more-under-obama-than-under-bush/.

GET RID OF THE NORTH AMERICAN FREE TRADE AGREEMENT—NAFTA

- United States Census Bureau, U.S International Trade Data, http://www.census.gov/foreign-trade/balance/c2010.html#2014).
- Patrick J. Buchanan, "Free Trade and Funny Math," Buchanan.org, February 27 2007, http://buchanan.org/blog/pjb-free-trade-and-funny-math-678.

BRING BACK "MADE IN THE USA"

- Greg Autry, "An Eyes Wide Open Look at U.S. Manufacturing," the Huffington Post, December 31 2012, http://www.huffingtonpost.com/greg-autry/eyes-wide-open-look_b_2388456.html.

SAVE SOCIAL SECURITY AND MEDICARE

- N.C. Aizenman, "Social Security's Financial Forecast Gets Darker; Medicare's Outlook Unchanged," Washington Post, April 23 2012, http://www.washingtonpost.com/national/health-science/social-securitys-financial-forecast-gets-darker-medicares-outlook-unchanged/2012/04/23/gIQA6hdQdT_story.html.

RAISE THE MINIMUM WAGE

- Clare O'Connor, "Report: Walmart Workers Cost Taxpayers $6.2 Billion In Public Assistance," Forbes, April 15 2014, http://www.forbes.com/sites/clareoconnor/2014/04/15/report-walmart-workers-cost-taxpayers-6-2-billion-in-public-assistance/.

SAVE THE MIDDLE CLASS

- Catherine Dodge and Mike Dorning, "Rich-Poor Gap Widens to Most Since 1967 as Income Falls,"

Bloomberg.com, September 12 2012, http://www.bloomberg.com/news/2012-09-12/u-s-poverty-rate-stays-at-almost-two-decade-high-income-falls.html.

- Ashley C. Allen, "Countries with the Widest Gap Between Rich, Poor," USA Today, May 21 2014, http://www.usatoday.com/story/money/business/2014/05/21/rich-poor-widest-gap/9351639/.
- Hope Yen, "Rich Poor Employment Gap Now Widest on Record," the Huffington Post, September 16 2013, http://www.huffington-post.com/2013/09/16/rich-poor-employment-gap_n_3933757.html
- Roberto A. Ferdman, "The Pay Gap Between CEOs and Workers Is Much Worse Than You Realize," the Washington Post, September 25 2014, http://www.washingtonpost.com/blogs/wonkblog/wp/2014/09/25/the-pay-gap-between-ceos-and-workers-is-much-worse-than-you-realize/.

STOP THE DOPING OF AMERICA'S CHILDREN

- Robert Whitaker, *Mad In America* (New York: Perseus Publishing, 2002).
- Dr. Peter R. Breggin, *Toxic Psychiatry* (New York: St. Martin's Griffin, 1994).
- Stephen H. Behnke, Michael L. Perlin, and Marvin Bernstein, *The Essentials of New York Mental Health Law* (New York: W.W. Norton & Company, 2003).

GET OFF FOSSIL FUELS

- Human Rights Watch, World Report 2013/Saudi Arabia

INVEST IN CLEAN ENERGY—SOLAR, WIND, WATER

- United States Department of the Interior, Bureau of Reclamation, Lower Colorado Region, Hoover Dam Frequently Asked Questions and Answers, "Hydropower at Hoover Dam," http://www.usbr.gov/lc/hooverdam/faqs/powerfaq.html

IMMEDIATELY RELEASE ANYONE INCARCERATED FOR A NON-VIOLENT DRUG CRIME

- Adam Liptak, "U.S. Prison Population Dwarfs that of Other Nations," New York Times, April 23 2008, http://www.nytimes.com/2008/04/23/world/americas/23iht-23prison.12253738.html?pagewanted=all&_r=0

INSTITUTE A 5 YEAR MAXIMUM JAIL SENTENCE ON NON-VIOLENT CRIMES

- Edwin Meese III, "The Constitution and Crime," Heritage Foundation, September 15 2010, http://www.heritage.org/research/commentary/2010/09/the-constitution-and-crime

EMBRACE OUR JUDEO-CHRISTIAN HERITAGE

- United States Department of the Treasury, History of "In God We Trust," http://www.treasury.gov/about/education/Pages/in-god-we-trust.aspx.
- Mildred Amer, "House and Senate Chaplains," CRS Report for Congress, April 2008, http://www.senate.gov/reference/resources/pdf/RS20427.pdf.
- Joanna Lin, "Bible Has a Storied Role in Inaugurations," LA Times, January 2009, http://articles.latimes.com/2009/jan/18/nation/na-inaug-religion18.
- Office of the Chaplain, United States House of Representatives, First Prayer of the Continental Congress, 1774, http://chaplain.house.gov/archive/continental.html.

GET RID OF POLITICAL CORRECTNESS

- Michael Moore, *Stupid White men—and Other Sorry Excuses for the State of the Nation* (New York: HarperCollins, 2001).
- Kim R. Holmes, "Charlie Hebdo, Intolerance, and the Problem of Double Standards," Heritage.Org, February 2015, http://www.heritage.org/research/commentary/2015/2/charlie-hebdo-intolerance-and-the-problem-of-double-standards.

CONFRONT AND DESTROY RADICAL ISLAM

- James Jay Carfano and Jessica Zuckerman, "40 Terrorist Plots Foiled Since 9/11: Combating Complacency in the Long War on Terror," Heritage Foundation, September 7 2011, http://www. heritage.org/research/reports/2011/09/40-terror-plots-foiled-since-9-11-combating-complacency-in-the-long-war-on-terror
- www.thereligionofpeace.com.
- Kevin Flower, "Rights groups decry Gaza 'Honor Killing'," CNN.com, July 30, 2009, http://www.cnn.com/2009/WORLD/meast/07/30/mideast.honor.killings/index.html.
- Irshad Manji, *The Trouble with Islam Today* (New York: St. Martin's Griffin, 2003), 25.
- Mohammed Jamjoom and Saad Abedine, "Saudi judge refuses to annul marriage of girl, 8," CNN.com, December 24, 2008, http://www.cnn.com/2008/WORLD/meast/12/23/saudi.arabia.child.marriage/index.html.
- Robert Spencer, *The Politically Incorrect Guide to Islam and the Crusades* (Washington: Regnery, 2005), 102.
- Pew Research Center, Pew Global Attitudes Project, "The Great Divide: How Westerners and Muslims View Each Other," June 22, 2006, http://pewglobal.org/reports/display.php?ReportID=253.

- Laura Ingraham, *Power to the People* (Washington DC: Regnery, 2007) 86.
- Jacob Poushter, "In nations with significant Muslim populations, much disdain for ISIS," Pew Research Center, November 17, 2015, http://www.pewresearch.org/fact-tank/2015/11/17/in-nations-with-significant-muslim- populations-much-disdain-for-isis/.
- Samuel P. Huntington, *The Clash of Civilizations and the Remaking of World Order* (New York: Simon & Schuster, 1996).

USE PROFILING WHEN NECESSARY TO PROTECT THE NATION AND SAVE LIVES

- Jessica Zuckerman, Steven Bucci, and James Jay Carafano,"60 Terrorist Plots Since 9/11: Continued Lessons in Domestic Counterterrorism," Heritage Foundation, July 22 2015, http://www.heritage.org/research/reports/2013/07/60-terrorist-plots-since-911-continued-lessons-in-domestic-counter-terrorism.

FIND AND SECURE ALL "LOOSE NUKES"

- Peter Grier, "Nuclear Summit: How Much 'Loose Nukes' Material is Out There?," Christian Science Monitor, April 13 2010, http://www.csmonitor.com/USA/Foreign-Policy/2010/0413/Nuclear-summit-How-much-loose-nukes-material-is-out-there.

STAND UP TO CHINA

- Spencer Ackerman and Jonathan Kaiman, "Chinese Military Officials Charged with Stealing US Data as Tensions Escalate," the Guardian, May 20 2014, http://www.theguardian.com/technology/2014/may/19/us-chinese-military-officials-cyber-espionage.
- Doug Palmer, "Senators Renew Push Against China Currency 'Manipulation' Despite Yuan's Rise," Reuters, June 5 2013, http://www.reuters.com/article/2013/06/05/us-usa-china-currency-idUSBRE-9541HY20130605.
- Human Rights Watch, World Report 2014/China, http://www.hrw.org/world-report/2014/country-chapters/china.

REQUIRE UNIVERSAL BACKGROUND CHECKS AND GUN SAFETY TRAINING

- Scott Clement, "Does the NRA Agree with Wayne LaPierre?," The Washington Post, January 31 2013, http://www.washingtonpost.com/news/the-fix/wp/2013/01/31/nra-leadership-members-divide-on-universal-background-checks/.

CREATE A "PEOPLE'S VETO" FOR SUPREME COURT DECISIONS

- Abraham Lincoln, "First Inaugural Address," in *Our Nation's Archive: The History of the United States in Documents*, ed. Erik Bruun and Jay Crosby (New York: Black Dog & Leventhal Publishers, 2009), 346.
- Mark R. Levin, *The Liberty Amendments* (New York: Simon & Schuster, 2013).

AMEND THE CONSTITUTION TO PROVIDE A "STATE'S VETO" OVER FEDERAL LEGISLATION

- Mark R. Levin, *The Liberty Amendments* (New York: Simon & Schuster, 2013).

PASS A LAW BANNING COMPLICATED LAWS

- Penny Starr, "Under Obama, 11,327 Pages of Federal Regulations Added," cnsnews.com, September 10 2012, http://cnsnews.com/news/article/under-obama-11327-pages-federal-regulations-added.

FIGHT!

- Mark R. Levin, *Liberty and Tyranny* (New York: Simon & Schuster, 2009).

- Michael Savage, Liberalism Is a Mental Disorder (Nashville: Thomas Nelson, 2005).
- David McCullough, *1776* (New York: Simon & Schuster, 2005).

PRAY

- The Bible
- Abraham Lincoln, Gettysburg Address, November 19, 1863.

AUTHOR BIOGRAPHY

Timothy M. Rosen received his juris doctor from St. John's University School of Law. He's a professor of law and ethics at Queens College of the City University of New York and an attorney in private practice. He has written for several outlets, including WorldNetDaily.

Raised in his native New York City, Rosen has experienced poverty firsthand and knows what it takes to overcome. That personal experience heavily influences his work and writing.

In his personal life, he is a die-hard Yankees fan and a Civil War buff. You can follow Rosen on Twitter at @RosenIsRight.